THE ENCYCLOPEDIA OF
MUSICAL INSTRUMENTS

KEYBOARD
INSTRUMENTS
& ENSEMBLES

Produced by Carlton Books Limited

20 Mortimer Street

London, W1N 7RD

Text and Design copyright © Carlton Books Limited 2001

First published in hardback edition in 2001 by Chelsea House Publishers, a subsidiary of

Haights Cross Communications. Printed and bound in Dubai.

First Printing

1 3 5 7 9 8 6 4 2

The Chelsea House World Wide Web address is http://www.chelseahouse.com

Library of Congress Cataloging-in-Publication Data applied for

Woodwind and Brass Instruments ISBN: 0-7910-6091-8

Stringed Instruments ISBN: 0-7910-6092-6

Percussion and Electronic Instruments ISBN: 0-7910-6093-4

Keyboard Instruments and Ensembles ISBN: 0-7910-6094-2

Non-Western and Obsolete Instruments ISBN: 0-7910-6095-0

THE ENCYCLOPEDIA OF
MUSICAL INSTRUMENTS

KEYBOARD INSTRUMENTS & ENSEMBLES

ROBERT DEARLING

Chelsea House Publishers

Philadelphia

THE ENCYCLOPEDIA OF
MUSICAL INSTRUMENTS

KEYBOARD INSTRUMENTS & ENSEMBLES

Woodwind and Brass Instruments

Stringed Instruments

Percussion and Electronic Instruments

Non-Western and Obsolete Instruments

CONTENTS

Keyboard Instruments

Keyboard instruments have been in existence since pre-Christian times. They come in all shapes and sizes and produce sound in different ways. Organs, the most ancient keyboard instruments, are wind machines; harp-sichords pluck strings; and pianos hammer. The keyboard instruments found in this section are of the closed case type. Open uncased variants, such as marimbas, vibraphones and xylo-phones, will be found under Percussion. The principal keyboard instruments of the renaissance and baroque were the harpsichord, virginal, spinet and clavichord. Generically, like the piano, all can be classified as chor-dophones of the boarded *zither* family. In the first three (effectively keyboard psalteries) the strings are set into vibra-tion by being plucked mechanically. In the clavichord, they are excited by brass tangents. The layout of strings custom-arily defines the identity of the plucked examples. In a virginal, they run roughly parallel to the keyboard. In a spinet, they run away diagonally to the right. In a harpsichord, they run directly away. Virginals and spinets have single sets (choirs) of strings, and single keyboards (manuals). The harpsi-chord usually has two or three sets, with either one or two keyboards (or manuals).

EARLY KEYBOARDS

𝄢 Clavichord

Chronologically the oldest, and possibly derived from the ancient monochord (a string stretched across a resonator with the vibrating length, or pitch, determined by a movable bridge), the clavichord looks like a simpler form of the rectangular virginal, with the keyboard likewise displaced to the left. In the 15th century it was often known as either *monochordium* or *monacordo*; the earliest use of the term 'clavichord' dates from 1404. Italian examples from the 16th century (with projecting keyboards) were transverse-strung. German instruments from the 17th/18th centuries (with inset keyboards) were oblique-strung (right front to left back). The rear ends of the keys have tangents or blades which strike pairs of metal strings. To the right of the strike-point is the vibrating length (pitch) of the string which crosses a bridge that carries the vibrations to the soundboard. Cloth, or 'listing', damps that part of the strings to the left.

Clavichords may be 'fretted' (each string-pair being struck in succession by differently-placed tangents), or 'unfretted' (in which each string-pair gives only one note). Needing half as many strings again, an unfretted instrument is described by Johann Speth (*Ars magna consoni ed dissoni*, 1693): "each key has its own strings and not some [strings] touched by two, three, and even four keys". Players on unfretted clavichords were able to accommodate pieces in distant tonalities. Fretted instruments were more limiting. The clavichordist has direct control over dynamic loudness, depending (piano-like) on the force of the strike; and over changes in sound through varying pressure on the sustained key - making possible vibrato or *Bebung* effects, and impressions of 'swelling' tone. (*Bebung* is particularly unique – C. P. E. Bach indicated it, and Beethoven may even have tried to simulate it in his late piano sonatas.)

By the late 18th century, the compass of the clavichord was that of the harpsichord and piano (five octaves). Three-and-a-half to four (with the omission of some bottom chromatics - the so-called 'short octave') seems to have been the earlier norm. Originally a learning or practice aid, yet with an unexpectedly intense range of expressive possibilities, the intimate clavichord was the domestic instrument of the German-speaking lands from the 16th century onwards. But it was not until the 18th century, when it was already being challenged by the harpsichord and the piano, that it finally came into its own as a creative and performing tool, "ideal ... for solitary musical self-communion" (Helen Rice Hollis). It was the favourite *Empfindsamkeit* medium of C. P. E. Bach. He praised it in his *Versuch uber die wahre Art das Clavier zu spielen* (1754–62): "the clavichord and pianoforte enjoy great advantages over the harpsichord and organ because of the many ways in which their volume can be gradually changed". He even wrote a rondo in farewell to a specially loved example by Gottfried Silbermann (1781).

𝄢 FAR LEFT: A DETAIL OF A GERMAN CLAVICHORD.
𝄢 BELOW: A RECREATION OF A CLAVICHORD, BY THE DOLMETSCH WORKSHOP.

✼ Harpsichord

In appearance the harpsichord foreshadows the wing-shaped, wooden-framed grand pianos of the late 18th century. The principal element of the harpsichord's activating mechanism is a slender wooden fork-shaped jack fixed vertically to the back of the key. The jack carries in a pivoted tongue a plectrum of quill; originally this was of crow, raven, turkey or eagle primary wing/tail feathers, later of soft buff leather or plastic. Depressing the key releases a cloth damper from the string, raises the jack and forces the plectrum past the string, plucking it. A release mechanism lets the jack return to rest. Depending on the point at which the string is plucked, and the material of the plectra, different tone qualities can be obtained. The sound lasts while the key is depressed, but decays quickly. In the hands of a good player, sophisticated *legato* (joined) and *staccato* (detached) articulation are possible. Many baroque composers devised ingenious ways of implying sustained sound, not least through ornamentation and trills. Changes of dynamic are impossible, though, unless there are extra jacks, strings or other mechanics. When, on bigger instruments, changes of dynamic are possible, they are by nature terraced rather than graduated: a vivid example of such stratified dynamics, with boldly stepped contrasts of *forte* (loud) and *piano* (soft), is found in Bach's solo Concerto in the Italian Style (1735). The harpsichord's dynamic limitations were eloquently lamented by Couperin in the preface to his first book of *Pièces de clavecin* (1713): "The harpsichord is perfect as to its compass, and brilliant in itself, but as it is impossible to swell or diminish the volume of its sound, I shall always feel grateful to any who, by

the exercise of infinite art supported by fine taste, contrive to render this instrument capable of expression".

✼ Types of harpsichord

First mentioned in Padua in 1397 as a 'clavicymbalum', with the earliest surviving example made in Bologna in 1521, harpsichords have been built and presented in different ways, depending on place and period. Originally they were short and thick-cased, with a single manual; a double-manual is mentioned in 1514. Another two-manual instrument, described as 'a pair of virginals in one coffer with four stops', is listed in Henry VIII's Privy Purse expenses for 1530. Typically, 16th-century Venetian examples, with one (8 foot) or two (8 foot plus 4 foot) choirs, had slender bodies made of cypress wood, with decorated outer cases.

The 16th/17th century Flemish school, centred on the legendary Ruckers family of Antwerp (who also made virginals), favoured thicker, generally painted casework, double choirs, and, by the 1590s, un-coupled double-manuals. Hallmarked by a distinctive soundboard rose, Ruckers' highly-valued harpsichords were resonant, tonally balanced instruments, and especially popular in England and France. A beautifully-crafted, rebuilt and enlarged French version of Ruckers, with an elegantly lacquered or painted soundboard and body, was created at the end of the 17th century by the Blanchet family of Paris. The instruments of the Blanchet dynasty were celebrated; Couperin 'le Grand' owned one of their harpsichords. By the mid-18th century they had been appointed 'facteur des clavessins du Roi', and by 1827 they were making their

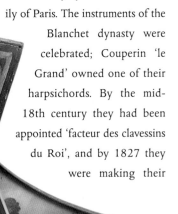

𝄞 A BEAUTIFULLY PAINTED HARPSICHORD OF PROBABLY 16TH CENTURY SOUTH GERMAN OR ITALIAN ORIGIN.

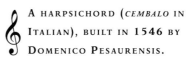

A HARPSICHORD (*CEMBALO* IN ITALIAN), BUILT IN 1546 BY DOMENICO PESAURENSIS.

first high-quality upright pianos. German harpsichords of the 18th century, principally from Hamburg, tended to be large and complex, with extra 2 foot (high) and 16 foot (low) registers, occasional pedal keyboards, and even (in one case, a Hass, made in 1740, with five choirs of strings) three manuals. Bach preferred such examples.

The English instruments of the 17th and 18th centuries were undecorated, oak or walnut veneered, and richly powerful with thicker soundboards. The most acclaimed makers of the 'English' type were the Swiss-born Burkat Shudi and the Alsatians Jacob and Abraham Kirkman. Shudi enjoyed exclusive patronage: from his friends Handel, Gainsborough and Reynolds to Haydn, Frederick the Great of Prussia and Maria Theresia of Austria. Among his inventions was the dubiously effective Venetian Swell (1769), designed to vary dynamic volume by the use of louvred wooden shutters (based on the Venetian blind idea). He also incorporated a 'machine stop' for quick changes in registration: a single (foot) pedal overriding individual hand stops and controlling several different registers of strings.

Broadly similar in specification, Kirkman's harpsichords were more numerous than Shudi's and had a virtual monopoly in London. Contrary to European tradition, the keyboards of English double-manual harpsichords were uncoupled in the Flemish style and produced harsh contrasts of timbre. This characteristic has often brought into question the suitability of 'English disposition' instruments to the mainstream continental harpsichord music of the baroque period.

❧ *The modern harpsichord*

Friedrich Heinrich Himmel is said to have played the harpsichord publicly in Berlin as late as 1805, with the Kirkman workshops making their last model in 1809. Together with the clavichord, the instrument was not to be heard again until Louis Diemer and Arnold Dolmetsch resurrected it

in the 1880s. The Parisian piano makers Pleyel and Erard revitalized interest as well, with the former exhibiting an instrument at the 1889 Paris Exposition. So, too, did Chickering in America, and Ibach and Neupert in Germany.

Like the modern piano, the early 20th-century harpsichord was largely a hybrid, bearing only a passing resemblance to its original form. Manufacturers went for size, sustaining power and projection, with more focus and less overtoning. It was usual to fit concert harpsichords with pedals rather than hand-stops to enable a quicker, more dramatically coloured response when changing registers. Treble strings were lengthened, bass ones were shortened and overspun with copper, as in the piano. Then, in 1923, Pleyel introduced a high-tensioned, iron-framed instrument – clearly an all-conquering, sensibility-attacking, jangling anachronism but one that nevertheless found favour with Wanda Landowska and her disciples – and for which Falla and Poulenc were to write their harpsichord concertos. Modern harpsichord making (and the construction kit industry) has largely reverted to period values, continental-style, as have most modern players.

AN EXAMPLE OF THE CRAFTSMANSHIP OF JACOB KIRKMAN, THIS HARPSICHORD DATES FROM 1756.

✄ Virginal

In a treatise of about 1460 the virginal is identified as "having the [rectangular, box-like] shape of a clavichord and [transverse] metal strings making the sound of a [small] harpsichord". The instrument was intended originally to be either placed on a table or held in the lap. English virginals generally followed Flemish design, with the keyboard either centred, or displaced, like the later 'square piano', to the left (called a 'spinett') or the right (called a 'muselar'). The spinett was bright in sound, the muselar rounded and flute-like. A more elaborate double model by Ruckers featured a small 'child' virginal at octave pitch, interfaced with a 'mother' virginal at unison pitch. They could be played separately or coupled. The origin of the name is unclear. "Like a virgin ... with a sweet and tranquil voice", says one 15th century source. Only "virgins played

 BELOW: AN ITALIAN VIRGINAL BY ONOFRIO GUARRACINO, DATED 1668.

on them" says another, 150 years later. Most representations show it played by young women (mostly standing, rarely seated). Copied out in 1606–19, the *Fitzwilliam Virginal Book* comprises 297 pieces by all the most eminent composers of the English virginalist school, including Bull, Byrd and Farnaby. *Parthenia or the Maydenhead of the First Musicke that ever was Printed for the Virginals, with works by William Byrd, Dr. John Bull and Orlando Gibbons*, was the first collection of keyboard music to be published in England, in 1613.

ABOVE: A MUSICAL PARTY SHOWING VIRGINALS AND FLUTE. IN ENGLAND FROM THE END OF THE 16TH CENTURY, 'VIRGINAL' WAS LOOSELY USED TO DESCRIBE ANY KIND OF QUILLED, PLUCKED KEYBOARD INSTRUMENT.

℅ *Spinet*

The spinet was another form of early domestic harpsichord, replacing the virginal. In French and Italian the term once defined any kind of small single-choir, single keyboard, plucked action instrument. Apart from outward shape, the principal difference between a virginal and a spinet is acoustic. In the former, both ends of the vibrating string length are supported by bridges on the soundboard. In the latter, which resembles a harpsichord, one end is supported by bridges fixed to the solid wrestplank – creating a fuller, firmer tone. German spinets of the 16th-century tended to be rectangular in design. Early 17th-century Italian ones were five or six-sided. 𝄢

Temperaments
℅

The octave is divided into twelve semi-tones. Depending on register, these vibrate at different frequencies (cycles per second), from slow (bass/low) to rapid (treble/high). Acoustically, modern 'equal temperament' (dividing the octave span uniformly) is impure in tuning (save for the octave interval) but allows free exchange, or modulation, between the major or minor keys (modes) of Western theory. Older 'mean tone temperament' (c. 1500) was purer in interval (notably thirds). In 'equal temperament' the black keys, or enharmonic 'accidentals' of the keyboard (C sharp/D flat, D sharp/E flat, F sharp/G flat, G sharp/A flat and A sharp/B flat) sound the same. But in 'mean tone temperament' there was an audible acoustic/frequency difference between each letter name. Theoretically, the major/minor scale patterns were shared. Practically, pitch was not (at least not without progressively unsatisfactory dissonance). In 'mean tone' tuning 'local' keys around C major were considered acoustically 'good'/possible for modulation, more 'distant' ones 'bad'/impossible, hence the restricted orbit of tonalities and key relationships found in so much Baroque and early Classical repertory. Depending on what key(s) they were playing in, string players could tune correspondingly to the 'mean' tone of the time, making slight but intonationally critical finger adjustments as necessary. Keyboard players were less fortunate, to such an extent that some harpsichords were even constructed with 'divided accidentals' so that each sharp and flat of the scale had its own string and key mechanism, giving seventeen keys to the octave (an unwieldy and expensive luxury).

'Equal temperament' solved the problem by splitting or 'tempering' the difference between sharps and flats, exchanging purity for practicality. Notwithstanding some modern disagreement, it is generally accepted that Bach's *Well Tempered Clavier* (two books, 1722; 1738–42) comprising 48 preludes and fugues, two in each of the major and minor keys, was the first work to comprehensively endorse the principle. Originally proposed in the 16th century, and strongly supported in the 18th by Rameau and C. P. E. Bach, the impurities of 'equal temperament' took time to get accepted. It was not until the mid-19th century that it was finally adopted in England and France. Now it is in general use, except in reconstructive 'period practice' playing where there has been a return to older temperament tunings.

A DOUBLE-MANUAL SPINET OF C. 1600 FROM THE FAMED WORKSHOP OF RUCKERS IN ANTWERP.

PIANO

Unlike the harpsichord or the clavichord, the piano is an equal temperament instrument in which the strings are struck percussively by rebounding hammers. Capable of graded dynamic contrasts depending on pressure of touch, its importance has been unchallenged for over two hundred years. No other modern acoustic instrument, apart from the organ, has such a wide frequency response from low to high, nor such expressive capacity, dynamic power, or colouristic possibility. Composers have used the piano to suggest a whole symphony orchestra. Arrangers have inventively used it to simulate one – from Czerny and Liszt to Mahler and the Second Viennese School.

A GRAND PIANO OF 1793 BY THE SOUTH GERMAN MAKER SEBASTIAN LENGERER OF KUFSTEIN.

Cristofori's Piano

Beethoven chauvinistically believed the piano to be a German invention, the powerful, all-encompassing post-Congress of Vienna Hammerklavier of his late sonatas. Given the pre-eminence of so many Austrian and German makers, many of them refugees of the Seven Years' War (1756–63), and the hammer action design of Christoph Schröter (without escapement), his presumption can be forgiven. Whatever the evidence for piano' prototypes (some going back to the 15th century), it was however not a German but a celebrated Paduan, Bartolomeo Cristofori, keeper of harpsichords and spinets at the court of Ferdinand de'Medici in Florence, who is traditionally credited with having invented the instrument – the first, an *arpicimbalo* (effectively a keyed dulcimer) around 1698–1700. Scipione Maffei went to Florence in 1709, and in his *Giornale dei letterati d'Italia* (1711) he mentions four "cleverly thought-out" Cristofori *gravicembali col piano e forte* ('harpsichords with soft and loud'), comparing their gradation of dynamic volume and power to that of the cello. Cristofori's pianos had paper-coiled, leather-covered hammers, and, innovatively, escapement action, which prevented the hammers rebounding onto the strings after the initial strike.

The Square Piano

In Germany the principle of Cristofori's Italian invention was taken up by the Freiberg organ-builder, Gottfried Silbermann. After some persuasion, J. S. Bach eventually came to admire and play his pianos, making suggestions for their improvement and even selling them. During his visit to the Potsdam court of Frederick the Great in 1747, he endorsed their assets publicly. Like Cristofori's, Silbermann's instruments were in the form of 'wing-shaped' grands. Many German makers, however, opted for the horizontal 'square' (oblong) clavichord-descended type, without escapement. An already sophisticated 'square' piano by Johann Socher, made in 1742, is the earliest surviving example of the type.

Piano Actions: German/Viennese vs English

During the latter half of the 18th century, two characteristic types of piano action evolved – the lighter 'German' and the heavier 'English' (fore-runner of the type familiar today). Based physically and aesthetically on the intimately expressive characteristics of Silbermann's pre-1750 clavichords, so beloved of C. P. E. Bach, 'German' *Prell-mechanik* action (with the hammer facing the player) was famous for its delicate touch and subtlety of nuance. Johann Andreas Silbermann of Strasbourg is credited with its invention, but it was left to his pupil, Johann Andreas Stein of Augsburg, extravagantly admired by Mozart and Beethoven, to perfect its damping and escapement elements, the former

Piano

NAMES

COTTAGE PIANO A small domestic upright marketed by Clementi and others in London early in the 19th century.

FLUGEL German for 'wing'. Both harpsichords and pianos are approximately wing-shaped.

FORTEPIANO An early name meaning 'loud-soft' (see Pianoforte), now reserved for early pianos, almost specifically those lacking full iron frames.

GRAND A horizontal piano, wing-shaped, with strings running diagonally away from the player.

HAMMERFLUGEL German. A wing-shaped instrument (keyboard by inference) in which the strings are struck by hammers.

HAMMERKLAVIER German for 'keyboard with hammers', as opposed to the plucked harpsichord. Beethoven specified a Hammerklavier for his late piano sonatas. In its narrow sense, *Hammerklavier* refers to a 'square' piano with hammers.

IVORIES Slang for piano (1855), referring to the material from which piano keyused to be made.

JOANNA (JOANO) English rhyming slang for 'piano' (1846).

KLAVIER German term for any keyboard instrument, but generally taken to mean 'piano'.

PIANOFORTE Italian for 'soft-loud', to distinguish the piano from the standard harpsichord, upon which graduated harmonics are not possible.

UPRIGHT A vertical piano for domestic use, rectangular in shape, with the strings running diagonally behind the keyboard.

controlled not by foot pedals but knee-levers.

In 1794 Stein's daughter, Nannette, set up business in Vienna with her husband J. A. Streicher: 'German' action became 'Viennese'. From this time until its closure in 1896, the firm of Streicher was the most important quality piano maker in Vienna. Their early instruments were favoured by all the great composers and virtuosos, from Beethoven to Hummel. Other eminent Austrian makers included Walter and Schantz (favoured by Haydn), Graf and (later) Bösendorfer.

❧ The 'English' Piano

Born in Saxony, Johannes Zumpe, who had served his apprenticeship in the workshops of Silbermann and Shudi, was predominantly responsible for the evolution of the 'English' piano during the reign of King George III. His earliest surviving trestle-supported single-action 'square' piano (without escapement) dates from 1766. Resembling a clavichord and largely tuned to an unequal temperament of 17 notes per octave, this had a small soundboard to the right, light hammers and reduced dynamic range. On 2 June 1768 Bach's youngest son, Johann Christian, the 'London' Bach, played a Zumpe instrument in the first solo performance on a piano in England. Zumpe's piano charmed English society. Its action was unsophisticated, and it was cheap to produce. Known on the continent as 'piano anglais', it made its way around the civilized world, reaching even as far as the harems of Ottoman sultans.

❧ Broadwood and the Grand Piano

In 1772 a Dutchman living in London, Americus Backers, helped develop 'English' grand or double-action (with escapement). Robert Stodart and

A SILBERMANN PIANO OF 1746, FROM AN ORIGINAL USED BY J. S. BACH AT THE COURT OF FREDERICK THE GREAT IN POTSDAM.

John Geib (another German) patented forms of it in 1777 and 1786 respectively. And the Scotsman John Broadwood (Shudi's son-in-law) improved its evenness, flexibility and dynamic power. Originally a joiner and cabinet maker, Broadwood was a visionary in piano design. He recognized that the optimum point at which hammer should strike string was critical in determining tone quality. In 1783 he patented foot-pedals; and in his redesigned 'square' pianos he introduced an under-damping mechanism. In 1788 he patented a divided bridge, with bass strings allocated a separate bridge (the long, single bridge of the harpsichord having formerly been customary). In 1818 Beethoven was sent a Broadwood grand (subsequently inherited by Liszt) that had a split damper pedal mechanism independently controlling bass and treble; Chopin played one during his final concerts in London and Manchester thirty years later. The family firm's instruments – according to a factory hand, "3,800 separate pieces of ivory, woods, metals, cloth, felt, leather and vellum, all fashioned and adjusted by hand" – were in wide demand in Victorian England, with an output of 2,500 a year by the 1850s.

SOUND & WORLDS

FRENCH, ENGLISH AND VIENNESE

A PIANOFORTE OF 1801 MADE BY THE FRENCH FIRM OF ERARD. BY THIS TIME ERARDS INCORPORATED THE ENGLISH ACTION.

Like Chopin, the Alsatian piano and harp maker Sébastien Erard preferred the greater volume and character of 'English' action instruments. He came to London in 1792, after fleeing the French Revolution, and opened a workshop. His first grand, improved 'English' style, appeared in 1796/7. Napoleon later owned one, and the great virtuoso Thalberg played them. Another illustrious French maker was the Austrian-born Ignaz Pleyel, in whose brilliantly lit Parisian concert room, the Salle Pleyel – graced by "a complete aristocracy of birth, wealth, talent and beauty" (Liszt) – all the greatest virtuosos of the Romantic age played. Apprenticed in London to Broadwood, Collard and Clementi, Pleyel's son Camille successfully carried on the family name.

As well as Broadwood, both Erard and Pleyel placed instruments at Chopin's disposal during his final stay in London. And it was on a Pleyel that Chopin completed his *Préludes* in Valdemosa, dedicating them to Camille. Like Field, Kalkbrenner and Gottschalk, he liked Pleyels for their "silvery and somewhat veiled sonority and their easy touch" (Liszt) and because they encouraged him "to find the sounds I want – when I am in good spirits and strong enough. When I am in a bad mood, I play Erard pianos and easily find in them a ready-made sound." Not so the American Edward MacDowell fifty years later. He likened Erard instruments – by then out of touch with progress and substantially more costly than any of their rivals – to be "a combination of wood and glass". Present-day French pianos – such as they are, for there are very few – are still thin-toned, a matter of national taste reflected no less in the crystalline character of Gallic keyboard writing – from Couperin 'le Grand' and Rameau to Ravel.

A BOSENDORFER COMMISSIONED FOR THE EMPRESS EUGENIE IN 1867. DESIGNED BY AUSTRIAN CRAFTSMAN HANS MAKART, IT HAS BURR, WALNUT AND ROSEWOOD MARQUETRY WITH BRASS INLAYS, AND CAST BRONZE STATUETTES.

❀ 'English' vs 'Viennese'

The different characteristics of 'Viennese' and 'English' pianos were tangible and audible. 'Viennese' action was shallower and easier, 'English' action, more resistant, deeper and harder. It 'pushed' rather than 'bounced'. 'Viennese' instruments (a tenth of the weight of their 20th-century descendents) had the benefit of rapid articulation, utmost

clarity, minimum delay between action and sound, and quick damping. 'English' ones were slower in speech and repetition because it was necessary for keys to return fully to rest before re-activation. In sound 'Viennese' pianos were thinner and more neutral within, though not between, treble, tenor and bass registers. 'English' ones were fuller and more coloured, with the tone more evenly distributed, thereby lending melodies, as Hummel wrote, "a peculiar charm and harmonious sweetness". Each action produced its own type of performer, and even its own type of composer. Mozart and Haydn belonged to Stein and the 'Viennese' school, Clementi and Dussek to Broadwood and the 'English'. Beethoven bridged the two – and dreamt further.

℁ The Upright

The 'square' piano endured in the drawing rooms of the wealthy for much of the 19th century – especially in America. Robert Wornum of London began making examples of vertically strung upright pianos in the 1800s, calling them 'cottage'

Piano Music Firsts

℁

Styles of composition usually associated with the piano fall into three categories:

1. Those taken over from other mediums as the piano became popular; eg, ballade ('narrative song'), barcarolle ('Venetian gondolier song'), polonaise, prelude, scherzo, variations, waltz etc. – omitted here.
2. Those taken over from other instruments but rethought in the light of the piano's capabilities; eg, concerto, sonata.
3. Those taken by and from other instruments but evolved with the piano in mind.

ALBUMBLATT ('album leaf'), originally an intimate short piece for a friend's album. Beethoven's *Für Elise* (1808), may have originated as such. In 1854 Schumann published a collection of twenty *Albumblätter*.

BAGATELLE ('a trifle', something insignificant), a name first used by Couperin (1717) but taken over for far-from-insignificant works by Beethoven from 1801.

BERCEUSE ('lullaby') first used by Chopin (1843–4) and later by Liszt.

CONCERTO The first concertos written specifically for a 'Pian e forte' (pianoforte) were the six of J. C. Bach's Op. 7 set of 1770.

ECLOGUE ('pastoral piece'), a word used by Tomášek from 1807 for 42 piano pieces.

IMPROMPTU (literally an improvisation, but written out). Schubert's two collections (1827) are substantial 'studies' in sonata, rondo, variation, nocturne and other forms. The title of the first set was at the suggestion of the publisher Haslinger.

LYRIC PIECE ('songful piece'), the title of ten sets (1867–1901) by Grieg.

MORCEAU ('piece'; 'morsel'), equates with *Stück*.

NOCTURNE ('night piece'), a term used by Mozart, Haydn and others for vocal ensemble pieces or serenades ('evening music'). The first three of John Field's Nocturnes for piano were published in 1814; the first three of Chopin's (Op. 9) in 1832.

SONATA Lodovico Giustini wrote 12 Sonatas, Op. 1, in 1732, titling them *Sonate da cimbalo di piano e forte detto volgarmente di martelletti* ('Sonatas for harpsichord with soft and loud, familiarly with little hammers'), to distinguish the intended instrument from the hammerless harpsichord.

SONGS WITHOUT WORDS, the title of eight sets of piano miniatures (1829–45) by Mendelssohn.

STUDY or ETUDE Developed from such collections as Bach's *Clavier-Ubung* ('keyboard exercises', 1731–42) and Türk's *Clavierschule* (1789), the first musically self-contained studies/études were by Cramer (1804, 1810) and Clementi (1817–26). Moscheles, Chopin, Liszt, Czerny and Alkan concentrated the style.

STUCK ('piece'), literally a 'piece' of music. *Klavierstücke* means 'pieces for piano'.

---

pianos. His future designs for small parlour instruments included low 'piccolo' and taller 'cabinet' models. A neat 'portable grand' from 1801, by Hawkins of Philadelphia featured a folding keyboard and boxwood naturals, as well as a revolutionary part-metal frame. Thomas Jefferson owned one. In their most basic form, uprights resembled dark coffins with broken teeth, and their voice was basic, but they were convenient and popular. All the leading European and American firms built them, with Steinway taking credit, in 1863, for the first identifiably modern prototype. 𝄢

 LEFT: A CABINET PIANO OF **1825** BY CLEMENTI, INTENDED AS A COMPACT INSTRUMENT FOR THE PARLOUR.

THE MODERN PIANO

The technology of the modern piano was confirmed during the 19th century, with an emphasis on equality of sound, brilliance of execution, projection and staying power. There were two critical innovations: Pierre Erard's 'double-escapement' action, patented in 1821, an advancement "of priceless value for the [rapid] repetition of notes" (Moscheles); and the development of an integral single-piece cast-iron ring frame, to replace the weaker, jointed (metal-braced) wooden ones of former design.

Cast-iron framing was perfected in America - first in 1825 by Alpheus Babcock (who applied it to the 'square'), then in 1843 by Jonas Chickering of Boston (who rendered the same service to the grand). At the 1851 Crystal Palace Exhibition, Chickering's majestic pianos were

Transposing PIANO

Proficient musicians and skilled accompanists can transpose into any key at will. To help those who could not, 19th-century piano makers, taking advantage of equal temperament, designed the transposing piano. In 1808 Broadwood introduced a movable keyboard. Four years later Erard patented a circular, rotating design. There were other methods, too. Most simplified the task but still to the disadvantage of the instrument. Modern electronic keyboards usually come with comprehensive transposition facilities.

AN OVER-STRUNG YAMAHA GRAND. NOTE THE SOUNDBOARD UNDER THE STRINGS. (ALSO SEE PAGE 127)

sensationally received: "I never thought a piano could possess such qualities", declared Liszt. Heavier and less susceptible to temperature variation, continuous iron-casting allowed for greater stress, thicker strings, more power and loudness,

and more secure tuning. Attached to their lighter, wooden frames, which were increasingly prone to fracture and decay, the Viennese long resisted any form of iron-work, believing it would corrupt the subtle tone of their instruments. But by the 1870s continuous iron casting had become a universally adopted construction method.

Another far-reaching improvement, not entirely unrelated, was 'over-stringing' (or 'cross-stringing') – with the combined tension of the strings redistributed across the whole frame by fanning a bass set diagonally across another of treble and tenor. Previously instruments had simply been parallel-strung. The idea was European, although some turn-of-the-century English 'upright grands' (smallish pianos up-ended and placed vertically, tail uppermost in rectangular cases on legs, not unlike the earlier pyramidal or later 'giraffe' pianos) had incorporated diagonal bass stringing. It was Babcock, however, who appreciated its value, as did Steinway, whose New York patent (December 1859) for an iron-framed, over-strung, double-escapement grand, with Cristofori ancestry, English facets and Viennese-style touch sensitivity, effectively confirmed the essentials of the piano as we now know it. The exhibition medals that followed triumphantly marked a new supremacy in the field.

❧ *Piano Making*

For practically three centuries pianos have been made by anyone and everyone from master builders to backstreet garret hands. The modern 'iron-age' alone has seen the rise and fall of more than 600 manufacturers in the UK, over 300 in Germany and nearly the same number in the USA – of whom only a few still survive. Around 1910 these countries were producing 75,000, 120,000 and 370,000 examples a year respectively. By 1970 that output had dropped significantly – to just 17,000, 45,000 and 220,000 – in the face of growing competition from the Soviet Union (with 200,000) and Japan (273,000). Ten years later, world production stood at around 800,000, an increase of 45,000. Today, China is making about half-a-million pianos annually; while in South Korea, Young

AN ENGLISH UPRIGHT GRAND OF C. 1810 BY LONDON MAKERS JONES, RICE AND COMPANY.

IMPORTANT
Piano Makers
❧

BECHSTEIN This Berlin company was established in 1853. Hans von Bülow inaugurated their first grand in a concert that included the first performance of Liszt's B minor Sonata (22 January 1857). Schnabel believed that the distinction of a good piano lay in its neutrality of sound. For him Bechsteins met this criterion ideally. Opened in 1901, the Bechstein Hall in London later became the Wigmore Hall.

BLUTHNER Founded, like Bechstein, in 1853, this Leipzig company is noted for its unusual, occasionally controversial, use of aliquot scaling to enrich the upper register (a 'sympathetically vibrating' fourth string added to each trichord treble, patented in 1873). Still largely made by hand, Blüthners have a silvery, romantic tone that arguably projects less well in bigger concert halls.

BOSENDORFER Originally this Austrian company, founded in 1828, only produced Viennese-action grands, but late in the 19th century they began to make English-action concert instruments. Bösendorfer's richly over-toned eight-octave Imperial Grands are among the most aristocratic instruments around, with a limpid clarity of sound and a bass response of profound gravity. Liszt, the great Viennese Romantics, royal patrons, and (in 1936) the BBC all helped establish the instrument's pedigree. Its devotees since have included Alfred Brendel and Oscar Peterson, Andras Schiff and Jools

Holland. Bösendorfers are exclusive: in 1828 only four were made, in 1990 just 600.

STEINWAY The pre-eminent concert piano: powerful, richly characterful, resonant. Founded, like Bechstein and Blüthner, in 1853 (in New York, with a Hamburg branch in 1880), Steinway perfected the modern grand and upright. "A Steinway," Paderewski claimed, "is always singing, no matter who plays it". The company's early marketing initiative was breathtaking. They courted nobility – from the Queen of Spain and the Empress of Russia to Queen Victoria and the Sultan of Turkey, along with a passing clutch of Rothschilds. They won over Liszt and Wagner. And, with Anton Rubinstein they toured their grands across the cities and heartlands of gun-law America, paying him $43,000 in gold for the privilege. Steinway thought big, made big, did big. They have not changed.

YAMAHA Japan's principal piano maker (together with Kawai, founded in 1925). Its first upright appeared in 1900, its first grand fifty years later. Yamaha enjoyed no early accolades, but now, with their reliably robust, bright, American-styled concert grands enjoying the endorsement of legendary pianists like Sviatoslav Richter, and sales flourishing, it is a different story. Constantly innovating and developing, Yamaha are the world leaders in synthesizers and digital electronic pianos.

Chang, a company boasting the largest piano factory in the world, claims a yearly turnover of around 150,000 uprights and grands.

Unlike violins, old pianos are particularly susceptible to damp, temperature variations, central heating, dust in the overspun coils of the strings, in addition to mechanical wear-and-tear and worn-out felts. They either fall apart or their soundboards (in essence, their hearts and souls) crack open. Some good instruments from before the First World War (especially those built by Steinway) linger on, but generally the best vintage pianos today are German-built from the 1920s and 1930s – when craftsmen in touch with older, traditional skills of instrument-making were still around. 𝄢

The Performers

JAZZ PIANISTS

❧

"Jazz came to America 300 years ago in chains," wrote the band-leader Paul Whiteman in 1926. To George Gershwin, jazz was the whole pent-up energy of the New World, the blood and pulse of slaves and outcasts. During the late 19th century the ivories and ebonies of the piano bridged in a curious way the segregation and split values of American society.

SCOTT JOPLIN, the 'King of Ragtime', son of a slave, the Schubert of the Mississippi nightlands. His celebrated *Maple Leaf Rag* (1899) and *The Entertainer* ('a ragtime two step', 1902) have been favourably compared to the popular dances of Mozart, Chopin and Brahms.

JELLY ROLL MORTON, self-styled 'inventor of jazz' from New Orleans with a weakness for women and diamonds. He was famous for his sense of rhythm and syncopation, and for how he developed the jazz 'break'. He never forgot the Latin/Creole roots of his birth ("if you can't manage to put tinges of Spanish in your tunes, you'll never get the right seasoning for jazz"), nor the fact that his pale skin made him a 'white' black.

DUKE ELLINGTON, Cotton Club pioneer of big band 'jungle' jazz, who claimed: "I don't write jazz, I write Negro music". He was a formidable pianist in his later years.

FATS WALLER, the 'Black Horowitz', wrote around 400 pieces. He made nearly 500 recordings, and cut many piano rolls. Inventive and diverse, he not only composed and played the piano and organ, but sang, was a band-leader and appeared in films. He used his humour to communicate in the most spectacular way. His exuberant pianism, rich in right-hand dazzle and left-hand drive, was a heady mixture of ragtime, barrelhouse, authentic blues, Harlem stride and cabaret.

COUNT BASIE, master of the 'riff', started out in vaudeville and had some informal piano lessons from Fats Waller. The Count Basie Orchestra, formed in 1937, was the leading Big Band of the 'swing' era.

🎼 DUKE ELLINGTON – "BACH
   AND MYSELF WRITE WITH THE
   ... PERFORMER IN MIND."

EARL HINES, the so-called 'father of jazz piano', served his apprenticeship in Chicago, and was closely associated with Louis Armstrong – with whom he recorded *Weatherbird* in 1928, perhaps the most celebrated duet in jazz history. Bridging blues, folk, pop, romantic/impressionist art-music and Hollywood, Hines was one of the undisputed kings of his world.

ART TATUM was the highest octane nightclub soloist of his generation, the pianistic phenomenon of the Big Band age. Informed, inventive and imaginative, he gave jazz piano a completely new dimension. His cast-iron technique, and his powers of transcendental improvisation, caused Fats to liken him to God.

THELONIOUS MONK was a pioneering 'bop' pianist in 1940s New York. Master of crushed notes, chord clusters and percussive dissonances, poet of anguish and silence, his lack of early piano training made for a characteristically flat-fingered technique. Since his death, he has acquired a considerable cult following.

DAVE BRUBECK studied with Milhaud, and has been a leading 'white' force in the experimental jazz scene since his West Coast days. "Jazz," he says, "is about the only form of art existing today in which there is freedom of the individual without loss of group contact".

OSCAR PETERSON, a Canadian, made his Carnegie Hall debut in 1949. As a jazz pianist of flawlessly natural technique, and as an informed jazz 'teacher', historian, and media presenter, his reputation worldwide is formidable.

CLASSICAL PIANISTS

❧

WOLFGANG AMADEUS MOZART (Austrian) — "It is much easier to play a thing quickly than slowly: in certain passages you can leave out a few notes without anyone noticing it. But is that beautiful? ... [you ought to be able to play a] piece in the time [tempo] in which it ought to be played, and [play] all the notes, appoggiaturas and so forth, exactly as they are written and with the appropiate expression and taste, so that you might suppose that the performer had composed it himself."

LUDWIG VAN BEETHOVEN (German) "Nobody equalled him in the rapidity of his scales, double trills, skips, etc – even Hummel. His bearing while playing was masterfully quiet, noble and beautiful, without the slightest grimace (only bent forward low, as his deafness grew upon him); his fingers were very powerful, not long, and broadened at the tips ... In teaching he laid great stress on a correct position of the fingers (after the school of Emanuel Bach, which he used in teaching me); he could scarcely span a tenth. He made frequent use of the pedals ... [more] than is indicated in his works" – Czerny

FRANZ LISZT (Hungarian) – "The virtuoso is not a mason who, chisel in hand, faithfully and conscientiously whittles stone after the design of an architect ... [Rather] he is called upon to make emotion speak, and weep, and sing, and sigh ... He creates as the composer himself created, for he himself must live the passions he will call to light in all their brilliance."

LOUIS MOREAU GOTTSCHALK ('The First American') "There is an exquisite grace in his manner of phrasing sweet melodies and scattering the light passages from the top of the keyboard" – Berlioz

ANTON RUBINSTEIN (Russian) "For every possible mistake he may have made, he gave, in return, ideas and musical tone pictures that would have made up for a million mistakes" – Rachmaninov

IGNACY JAN PADEREWSKI (Polish) "[The] most legendary pianist after Liszt ... The man had style and a big heart; and he had immense dignity and glamour; and he could produce golden sounds; and he was an unparalleled showman. And so while his competitors were counting his wrong notes, he was counting his dollars" – Harold C. Schonberg

LEOPOLD GODOWSKY (Polish-American) "The superman of piano playing. Nothing like him, as far as I know, is to be found in the history of piano playing since Chopin ... a pianist for pianists" – James Huneker

SERGEI RACHMANINOV (Russian) "By the time [Rachmaninov] has gone through a long work we know all, or nearly all, that it is possible for a piano musically to express ... he concentrates his essences in the chalice of style ... the aristocrat of pianists" – Neville Cardus

ARTUR SCHNABEL (Austrian-American) – "To buy a ticket [to a concert] is no insurance of happiness. The performer only promises to try his best, but he cannot promise to please the listener."

ARTHUR RUBINSTEIN (Polish-American) – "I was chastened [by critics] for my 'severe' interpretations of Chopin. Stubbornly I continued programming Chopin... stubbornly the critics continued to criticise ... Only very much later was the validity of my interpretation granted. Only then was I permitted to have my Chopin and to give him to audiences."

CLAUDIO ARRAU (Chilean) – "I don't believe in an afterlife, so whatever is, is right here and now ... That is why I have stressed the building of one's own structure and one's own vision based on truth, on fidelity to the composer's text. That is my legacy."

VLADIMIR HOROWITZ ('The Last Romantic', Ukrainian-American) – "A pianist is a citizen of the world. And that is the most important thing to be."

CLIFFORD CURZON (British) – "I wonder if many people ... realise the crucial importance of fingering? You've only got ten fingers, and you've got nearly one hundred keys. And it's the arrangement of those ten fingers, and the way each follows the other, that not only allows you to play the right notes, but lets you shape the music, and make it speak."

SVIATOSLAV RICHTER (Russian) "An inspired poet of music and in that is his mesmerising power ... I caught myself thinking that I was witnessing an exceptional phenomenon of the 20th century" – Rosina Lhevinne

DINU LIPATTI (Rumanian) "An artist of divine spirituality" – Poulenc

ALFRED BRENDEL (Austrian) – "Records are a kind of offspring of which one can't, unfortunately, say that one has to nurse them until they grow up and then forget them as soon as possible and let them lead their own lives. They lead their own lives at once, and are scarcely ever grown up! There's always something infantile about a record, at least as far as the artist is concerned. Records are interesting to learn from – but not always to enjoy."

GLENN GOULD (Canadian) – "Music is something that ought to be listened to in private. I do not believe that it should be treated as group therapy or any other kind of communal experience. I think that music ought to lead the listener – and, indeed, the performer – to a state of contemplation, and I don't think it's really possible to attain that condition with 2,999 other souls sitting all around ... I don't much care for piano music."

VLADIMIR ASHKENAZY (Russian-Icelandic) – "The concert pianist must devote all his life and all his time to music. Style, technique, meaning, and interpretation are not accidental qualities that just seem to fall into place at a given time; they are the result of practice and concentration [and] a lot of hard work."

MAURIZIO POLLINI (Italian) "Complete supremacy" – Artur Rubinstein

SVIATOSLAV RICHTER — FORMIDABLY TALENTED RUSSIAN VIRTUOSO OF WIDE REPERTORY.

THE CONCERT GRAND

THEN AND NOW

THE MODERN CONCERT piano is a durable, heavy-weight, high-tensioned, high-performance, scientifically optimized, individually crafted, voiced and regulated machine of nearly 12,000 parts, more than capable of holding its own against an orchestra. Today's grand is a radically different proposition from its 18th-century prototype. Its compass is expanded: up to eight octaves (Bösendorfer imperial) compared with Cristofori's four-and-a-half. Its action is heavier and more muscular. Beethoven's and Weber's brilliant octave work and *glissandi*, not to mention Liszt's or Brahms's, were envisaged for something much lighter and shallower. Steel and copper strings (thicker, tougher) have replaced brass and wire thread (thiner, brittler).

According to time and place, pitch has changed. Today's concert A (above middle C) is standardized at 440 Hz (cps), as agreed in 1939, and again in 1955. Stein's tuning fork, which Mozart knew, gave a reading of only 421.6 (1780), about the same as Handel's. In London, Broadwood favoured changing pitch according to purpose – from 434 (pianos accompanying voice) to 452.5 (pianos with instruments) or even higher (455.5). Chopin's recital A was fixed at 449. Elsewhere in Europe measurements differed, sometimes radically so. In France in 1859, A was established at 435 (diapason normal); in Dresden it stood at 441; in Liszt's Weimar at 444.7; in Leipzig at 448.7; in Prague at 449.7; in St Petersburg at 451.5; in Berlin at 451.7; in Vienna at 456. Across the Atlantic it was raised further: in 1879 Steinway tuned their A to 457

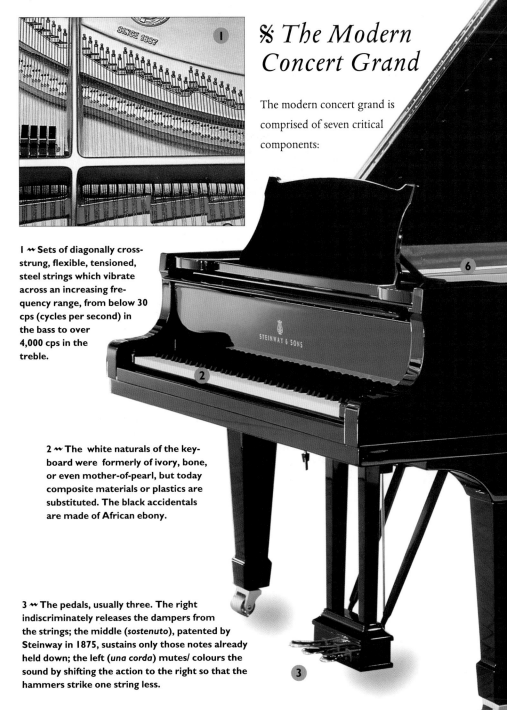

❧ The Modern Concert Grand

The modern concert grand is comprised of seven critical components:

1 ∾ Sets of diagonally cross-strung, flexible, tensioned, steel strings which vibrate across an increasing frequency range, from below 30 cps (cycles per second) in the bass to over 4,000 cps in the treble.

2 ∾ The white naturals of the keyboard were formerly of ivory, bone, or even mother-of-pearl, but today composite materials or plastics are substituted. The black accidentals are made of African ebony.

3 ∾ The pedals, usually three. The right indiscriminately releases the dampers from the strings; the middle (*sostenuto*), patented by Steinway in 1875, sustains only those notes already held down; the left (*una corda*) mutes/ colours the sound by shifting the action to the right so that the hammers strike one string less.

4 ⤳ **A wooden case (ebonized, veneered, lacquered, poly-ure-thaned), and bracings that can have the effect of a secondary soundboard. The lid acts as a directional sound reflector.**

Hz – gaining brightness in the process but at the expense of greater stress on the frame. Old instruments cannot withstand such high tensions: period practice performances, therefore, usually revert to lower pitch (pre-1800) tunings, with A averaging around 430 for Classical works and 415 for Baroque repertory.

Modern pedalling possibilities are less varied. A true una corda, for example – striking just one string with a proportionately dramatic change in

volume and timbre – can only be managed on old 'English' action instruments. Modifying the sound even further, the *sourdine* or mute-stop (moderator) of 'Viennese' actions – a piece of felt between the strings and hammers, originally activated by hand-stops – is likewise no longer available. Nor, too, is the (dry, soft) lute-stop. Other early colouristic effects – 'Turkish music' ('Janissary'), bassoon and harpsichord stops, for instance – have similarly long since disappeared. Their transmogrifying principle of making the piano what it was not – of contriving or distorting other timbres by making drumsticks, for instance, strike the underbelly of the soundboard, or using foreign materials placed on or between the strings – has not been forgotten, though. 'Playing' the strings rather than the keyboard (Cowell's *The Banshee*, 1925), the 'prepared' piano sounds of Tudor, Crumb or Wolff, the nuts and bolts, screw and rubber prescription of Cage's *Sonatas and Interludes* (1946–8), and the piano 'preparations' of our own day are, in a sense, no different. All are a common denial of what we are aurally conditioned to expect.

The tonal palette of today's piano, as occasionally magnificent as it can frequently be impersonal, is not that of Mozart's or Beethoven's time, nor even of Liszt's wandering years of transcendental execution as Europe's greatest *klaviertiger*. Its focussed, brighter, metallic timbre, its facility to scale massive dynamic ranges and project sound, is a response to modern halls and modern excesses. Its ability to fake a 'singing' *legato* line may be better, but gone is the luminous, crystalline, stringy resonance of its thin-wired, buckskin-hammered ancestors. In the concertos of Mozart, where in the *tuttis* the instrument is expected to have an interactive continuo role, it almost always blends uneasily with the orchestra, no matter how sympathetic the artist. In such situations, only the thinnest, shallowest sounding instruments ever convince - those closest to the intimacy and transparency of the Steins and Streichers of the late 18th century 𝄢.

5 ⤳ **An internal cast-iron frame, bearing the aggregate tension of the strings (16–30 tons), which run from hitch pins (far end) to wrest (tuning) pins (near end).**

6 ⤳ **A soundboard, a thin, flexible wooden diaphragm, typically of seasoned Norwegian spruce. This transmits the vibrations of the strings and acts as a powerful resonator. (Also see illustration on page 122)**

7 ⤳ **A removable action of infinitely fine adjustment, consisting normally of an 88-note keyboard, felted hammers, felted gravity over-dampers, and a series of intricate operating mechanisms. The same keys equally activate hammers (which induce sound) and dampers (which silence it). To prevent hammers from rebounding back onto strings already struck, an 'escapement' mechanism is used.**

ORGAN

"There let the pealing Organ blow, / To the full voic'd Quire below, / In Service high, with Anthem cleer, / As may with sweetness, through mine ear, / Dissolve me into extasies, / And bring all Heav'n before mine eyes." – Milton, *Il Penseroso* (1632)

From the pre-Christian hydraulis (see page 230) and hand-held pagan syrinx or panpipes (originally dried-out plant stalks of varying diameter and length) (see page 190), to the gigantic seven-manual instruments of the New World with the massed force of 25 military bands, the organ has evolved to become the most complex, sonically awesome and technically demanding of all musical instruments. "There's nothing to it," Bach may have said, "you only have to hit the right notes at the right time and the instrument plays itself". Beethoven believed otherwise: "an organist who is master of his intrument [should be placed] at the very head of all virtuosi".

A POSITIVE ORGAN IS THE CENTREPIECE OF THIS ITALIAN BOOK PAINTING (C. 1350), BY BOETHIUS.

Early History

The organ has a long and ancient history, extending back to the 3rd century BC. Later, it was popular with the Romans: a surviving example from 228 AD has four ranks of thirteen bronze flue pipes (one open, three stopped). It was then forgotten until Byzantium revived interest in it during the 9th and 10th centuries, by which time pneumatic action had virtually replaced water. (Winchester Cathedral supposedly had one with 400 pipes and 26 bellows, calling for two organists at two keyboards of 20 notes each.) The Byzantines regarded the organ as a gilded and silvered instrument of royal gift – Charlemagne was a recipient.

By the 1400s the large organ had become an important feature in churches, with the Rhinelanders calling for two or three manual instruments (among the most mechanically

TYPES OF
Organ
℅

BARREL ORGAN (Hand organ) An English barrel-and-pin portable instrument with flue pipes and bellows, cranked by a handle and first advertised in London as early as 1772. Some were capable only of mechanical performance, but others included separate keyboards. Barrel organs usually had five stops and up to five interchangeable barrels pegged with tunes of the day, religious and secular. Barrel organs were to be found in many Anglican churches up to the 1950s. They were popular, too, in their street form – though not everyone appreciated them: "In this unmusical country," wrote the Princess Lieven to Metternich in July 1820, "there are dreadful barrel organs which go up and down the streets - there is one playing under my window right now, which is so out of tune that it almost makes me weep ..."

ORGUE DE BARBARIE Neither an organ of the Barbary coast nor a barbaric instrument but a corruption of the name of its late 18th-century Italian adaptor, possibly Barbieri. This instrument consists of a portable case with pipes of metal or wood, or both. A handle turns a barrel and feeds the bellows.

PORTATIVE ORGAN (*Organetto*) A small portable melody instrument of the late Middle Ages. Resting on the left knee, it was played by the right hand, with the left operating the bellows. "So beautiful that even the birds listened to it", it was frequently depicted in contemporary paintings as an instrument of angels.

POSITIVE ORGAN The organ is traditionally associated with size and mighty sound, but there have been plenty of smaller domestic examples. The positive was one such, a small semi-portable medieval chamber organ of reduced compass. It came with flue pipes (usually in two ranks of 4 foot and 2 foot), a single manual and no pedalboard. A smaller table-top model needed an assistant to work the bellows.

REGAL Another portable organ, this one popular in Germany in the 15th-17th centuries. The origin of the name is unclear; perhaps a corruption of 'reed', for the regal was a reed-pipe instrument (in contrast to the positive). Monteverdi used a regal in his opera *L'Orfeo* (1607). The Bible Regal was a very much smaller folding version.

advanced in Europe). The needs of the Italians and French were more modest: one manual, fewer than a dozen stops. (In Italy double manuals, reed stops and swell boxes were not to gain currency until the 18th century.) The English followed suit, though they showed more interest in evolving new flute and reed stops. By the 15th century it was customary for the wind-chests, pipes and operating mechanics of the organ to be enclosed in a fretworked, screened wooden case, with the keyboard(s) and stops centred in front. This case, which possessed important cavity resonances, pro-

tected the fragile mechanism of the instrument, blended the sound and projected it to the listener.

During the 16th and 17th centuries European instrument builders, composers and players increasingly became streamed into national organ schools, each with their own identity and preferences. The French were drawn to bold contrasts and imposing choruses (*plein jeu*, *grand jeu*), to well-differentiated colours and echoes, to flute mutations (*tièrce*), to reeds with brilliant tops and

robust bottoms. A typical Louis XIV organ of around 1650 was a characterful beast. Equally so were those silvered visions of the 18th century, built by men like Andreas Silbermann (brother of Gottfried) and Clicquot. In post-Reformation England (less single-minded), the influence of the French held sway until the 18th century. The adoption of the pedal-board and the replacement of the Choir by the Swell as principal second manual was not until the 1720s. 𝄢

THE CLASSICAL ORGAN

The Swiss emigré John Snetzler brought notably fine voicing to the Anglican baroque/classical organ, as well as a colourful (and prophetic) resource of European stops, the manual coupler and the tremulant (from *tremolante*, meaning 'with tremolo'). During the 1760s some of his most impressive commissions were undertaken for Buck House, Peterhouse Cambridge and Beverley Minster – a lasting legacy from George III's reign. Throughout the 18th century, continental-style English organs were regularly shipped to the Americas, to the flourishing 'English' schools in New York and Boston.

The Spanish 18th-century organ, originally modelled on the Flemish type, was distinctive for its horizontally projecting reed pipes. It was used for ceremonial occasions. The German chapel organ of Bach's time represented the golden age of the instrument. This technically sophisticated, highly ornate example of the builder's craft was designed to stimulate many kinds of possible registrations and effects, rather like its 17th-century Dutch secular predecessor. Placing a premium on power, albeit sometimes at the expense of finesse, and with makers of the standing of Silbermann and Casparini, the Germans decided the organ of the 18th-century organ.

❧ Compass

Paralleling the clavichord, harpsichord and fortepiano, the compass of the early 18th cen-

THE THREE-MANUAL, 45-STOP SILBERMANN ORGAN OF 1710–14, FREIBURG CATHEDRAL (SAXONY).

tury organ was less than it is today. Bach's German instruments, with a pedal-board short of the four highest notes, normally had only a four-octave manual compass (lacking the modern top octave). Handel's English examples, mostly without pedal-board, had a manual compass generally both lower and higher than Bach's.

Pitch, too, was different. Compared with modern concert A = 440 Hz (cps) – or the exceptionally high 506 of the organ of Halberstadt Cathedral, 1495 – Mattheson's in Hamburg (1762) measured 408, with the organ of Trinity College Cambridge lower still at 395 (1759).

Germany, England and France led the organ into the Romantic age, post-Waterloo (1815). Many old instruments were modified and added to as a result of gathering interest in Bach's organ works. Octave couplers, double pedal-boards and solo manuals became standard with larger models. By 1833 mechanical-pneumatic action ('Barker lever') was in use on English examples in England (as well as higher wind pressure and better swell boxes). It was left not to the Germans (they now of decadent effect, coarse sound and 'orchestral' exaggeration – witness their mania for monster music mechanalia) but a Frenchman, Cavaillé-Coll of Paris, to perfect the electric-powered, fully pneumatic tracker action organ of the later 19th century. Through innovative design and mechanical re-thinking, he unleashed unheard of volume and expressivity. He gave the instrument its modern flexibility. He also gave it access to many non-classical French traditions (from Spain and Germany, as well as England), forging on the way an entirely new hybrid. Cavaillé-Coll was the Steinway of the Romantic

organ, and composers from Franck and Widor to Poulenc and Messiaen gloried in the cocktail. Today the vogue is either for building costly new instruments in big concert-halls or for period reconstructions and restorations, with performer-consultants continuing to play their time-honoured role of advising and improving.

℅ *The Cinema or Theatre Organ*

This product of the early 1900s was the favourite musical accompaniment/intermission instrument of the picture house and seaside pier. Largely replacing the orchestral group, it produced a warm, excessively syrupy sound – a combination of vox humana and tremulant richly smeared. The 'Mighty Wurlitzer', introduced in 1910, was only one of many examples. Wurlitzer began in the same year as Steinway, 1853, and continue to be in the forefront of electronic organ production for domestic use. Like the German Hupfeld company, they made innumerable mechanical instruments, a number specifically for theatre, cinema or ice rink application (including photoplayers). Elaborately housed and keenly marketed, these were impressive performers with ear-catching mechanics. Contemporary with their theatre organs, the Model 32A Concert Pian-Orchestra, for instance (using pneumatic rolls), boasted an instrumentation of piano, 56 violins, 30 cellos, 30 violas, 26 saxophones, 30 flutes, 30 piccolos, 30 clarinets, 30 oboes, 26 French horns, 26 bass violins, chimes, bass and snare drums, triangle, tambourine, castanets, tremolo, kettledrum and cymbals. The cinema organ, with its whiff of smoky nostalgia and fancy tricks, remains popular with audiences. 𝄢

THE VETERAN ORGANIST GERALD SHAW PLAYING A FIVE-MANUAL CINEMA ORGAN.

SOUNDING PRINCIPLES

OF THE ORGAN

The organ is activated by pressurized air from a wind-chest, released by valves into sets (stops, registers) of different-sized and tuned pipes. One or more coupled five-octave 61-note normal pitch keyboards (manuals, C to c ''''), together with a 32-note foot pedal board, control the individual opening or shutting of these valves (known as pallets). Different stops can be drawn to sound several ranks of pipes together – thereby selecting, mixing, reducing or strengthening different tone-colours (registration). By depressing the manual or foot keys it is possible to open the valves in several ways.

℘ Types of Action

- ↝ Tracker (mechnical) action – wind gathered in the pallets is released to each stop (pipe row) by means of a perforated wooden slider. This directs or diverts (retires) the wind to/from the row.
- ↝ Tubular-pneumatic action – pressurized air in a touch-box above the keys flows along tubing to a pneumatic motor, controlling the pipe-chest valves.
- ↝ Electro-pneumatic action – considered the best means of controlling very large instruments. In this type the pallet is opened by a magnet.

℘ THE UPPER PART OF THE CONSOLE OF THE ORGAN IN WESTMINSTER ABBEY, LONDON, SHOWING MANUALS (FOUR) AND STOPS.

According to Charles B. Fisk, the American organ-builder, modern tracker action, characterized by its mechanical connections between keys and valves and low wind pressures, "retains a geometry and a tonal ideal already firmly established in the 17th century ... A well-built tracker action affords the player a sense of immediacy (through 'feedback') that is totally unattainable with electro-pneumatic action".

℘ The Pipes: Pitch and Voicing

The separately mounted pipe divisions are normally identified as Great Organ, Choir Organ, Solo Organ, and Pedal Organ, together with a manual Swell Organ (related to the Venetian blind principle of the harpsichord) allowing the volume to be graduated. Occasionally, these specifications can be varied. The 6,655-pipe organ of Norwich Cathedral (1899, rebuilt 1942, originally five manual), for example, includes primary and secondary Greats, an unenclosed Positive and enclosed Swell Choir Organ, Great Reeds and an Echo Organ.

The bodies, or resonators, of pipes come in various forms. Flue pipes are usually of tin, or a tin/lead alloy, or wood, with the air striking the edge of the upper lip. Reed pipes have beating reed tongues (brass) setting an air-column into vibration. In a flue pipe, pitch is determined principally by length (the longer the pipe, the lower the pitch), and tone quality is affected by the size of the flue (or wind passage), foot-hole bore, and positioning of the lip. In a reed pipe, pitch is determined by the length of the air column, and by the length, mass and flexibility of the reed.

Regulating and adjusting the timbre, attack and loudness of pipes is called 'voicing'. In flue pipes this affects the amount of air coming from

the wind passage, in reed pipes the curvature and mass of the reed tongue. Family groups of tone colour, controlled by keyboard console 'stop-knobs', are determined by scaling. This is the relationship between the diameter and length of the pipes. Wide-bore pipes are less overtoned and penetrating than narrow ones, which have a brighter tonal quality (principal tone or diapason). 'Principals' are open flue pipes. 'Flutes', which are wider scaled, are usually stopped at their upper end (which acoustically doubles the length of the body, lowering pitch by an octave). Reed pipes come in three kinds: chorus (trumpet, brass); semi-chorus (non-imitative baroque); and solo/orchestral (imitative of orchestral single/ double reed woodwind). Evocatively descriptive, stop names, largely standardized by the end of the 16th century, refer either to family identities and pipe construction, or the orchestral instruments they imitate.

℅ Pitch

The scalic pitch of a rank, or register, of pipes is customarily measured in feet, taken from the speaking length of the fundamental or lowest pitch (a terminology also adopted by harpsichord makers). A unison open flue stop with a speaking length of 8 feet, for instance - sounding the C fundamental two octaves below middle C (the lowest note of the manuals at normal pitch) - is known as an 8-foot stop, or Foundation Stop (Open diapason); 4-foot or 2-foot stops (Octave, Super-Octave Stops) sound the same pitch respectively an octave or two octaves higher. A 16-foot stop (Double Stop) will sound an octave lower. Most modern big organs, such as that of the London Royal Festival Hall's 1951 Harrison & Harrison, extend to 32 feet. However, the organ in Hull City Hall (1950 Compton recon-

BRIGHTLY PAINTED FLUE PIPES OF A FAIRGROUND ORGAN. THE PIPES ARE GRADUATED AS TO SIZE (AND HENCE PITCH).

struction) goes one better, to a rare 64-foot Gravissima Stop, giving a bottom infra-frequency outside human hearing (five octaves below middle C): the vibratory sensation of such a stop is physical rather than auditory. Mutation Stops are those which sound at a pitch or harmonic other than the fundamental or its octaves. Compound or Mixture Stops are those comprised of two or more ranks of pipes. The organ of Liverpool Cathedral has a ten-rank Mixture ('Grand Chorus'), giving ten pipes for each pitch, or 610 in all for a complete five-octave stop. An Acoustic (Resultant) Bass pedal Stop is one whereby the physiological phenomenon of a differential tone an octave lower than its possible fundamental (the Tartini Tones of the 18th century) is operated.

THE ORGAN IN PERFORMANCE

THE ORGAN has been associated with the Church since medieval times, much of its music having been written with either liturgical function, liturgical association or liturgical performance in mind. This is still the case – despite evidence that the orchestral, concerto and recital use of the instrument in the 19th and 20th centuries helped broaden and secularize its image. The fact remains, however, that an organ recital is more likely to take place in a cathedral or church than a concert hall, and that its programme will consist of pieces largely intended for such a spiritual ambience.

✳ Symphonies and Concertos

In sacred music of the Baroque and Classical periods, the organ usually played a continuo role within the ensemble, doubling the bass line and supporting or filling-in the harmonies. It is in such capacity that Bach wrote for it in his *B Minor Mass*, Handel in *Messiah*, Mozart and Haydn in their Latin masses, and Beethoven in the *Missa Solemnis*. Even Brahms, much later (1854–68), thought of it in this way in his Lutheran *German Requiem*. Some of Haydn's masses (for instance, the *Grosse Orgelmesse*, by 1774; the *Nelson*, 1798) give it an *obbligato* function, but its first really spectacular appearance – theatrically confronting orchestra and choir – does not seem to have been until Berlioz's *Te deum* (1849).

Between the period of the 1848 Revolutions and the First World War, eight key late-Romantic symphonies or symphonic-type works by five composers use the organ – either to evoke mood

and association, to command attention, to introduce a sense of (physically-felt) gravitational vibration, or to lend climactic finality to cadential perorations: Liszt's *Faust* Symphony (1854–7); Saint-Saëns' Third ('Organ') Symphony, 1886 – not to be confused with the pioneering unaccompanied organ-symphony tradition of Widor, qv);

Mahler's Second ('Resurrection', 1888–94); Richard Strauss's *Also sprach Zarathustra* (1895–6); Scriabin's *Poem of Ecstasy* (1905–8); Mahler's Eighth

Symphony (1906–7); Scriabin's *Prometheus, The Poem of Fire* (1908–10); and Strauss's 'Alpine' Symphony (1911–15).

The earliest organ concertos, a secular product of largely Protestant countries, were by J. S. Bach (unaccompanied, c. 1713–14, arranged from the music of other composers, including Vivaldi) and Handel (eighteen in all, published in London in three sets between 1738 and 1761). Scored for organ (without pedal-boards), strings and reed woodwind, and comprised of a tuneful if complex web of self-borrowings and quotations (notably from Telemann), these were intended originally to be played as interludes between the acts of Handel's odes and oratorios. Other contributions were made by Johann Gottfried Walther, Bach's cousin (1741; plus a number of transcriptions); Michel Corrette (Six Concertos, Op. 26, 1756), who was responsible for bringing the virtuosic Handelian organ style to France; Samuel Wesley (several, the first in 1776, also one on Arne's *Rule Britannia*, and another (in 1800) for solo organ and violin); and Soler, a pupil of Scarlatti (Six Double Concertos for Two Organs). Given the non-portable nature of an installed organ (orchestras had to come to it, and venues were fewer, less varied and, if consecrated, more liturgically restrictive than today), the 19th century witnessed a steep decline of interest in the medium. But the aloof Rheinberger did contribute a couple of concertos, the first in 1884.

The 20th-century concerto remains a selective genre, in spite of the modern phenomenon of the ecclesiastically independent virtuoso concert organist: Hindemith (*Kammermusik No. 7*, 1927; Organ Concerto, 1962); Dupré (First Symphony, 1928; Concerto, 1934); Poulenc (Concerto for Organ, Timpani and Strings, 1938); Petr Eben (1954; 1982); Malcolm Williamson (1961); Anton Heiller (1964; Concerto for Organ, Piano and Chamber Orchestra, 1972); Charles Chaynes (1966); Jacques Charpentier (Concerto for Positive Organ, 1970; Symphony No. 6, 1979); Charles Camilleri (1981). 𝄢

THE
Organ Symphony
※

Just as the symphony for solo piano was a French invention (Alkan's), so too was the symphony for solo organ. Multi-movemented, exploiting the whole awesome range, power and registration of the French Romantic organ as built and expanded by Cavaillé-Coll, the organ-symphony was the creation of Widor, an organist in the grand manner who ruled the organ-loft of St. Sulpice in Paris from 1870 to 1934. He wrote ten in all (1876–1900), with the Toccata finale of the Fifth enjoying special popularity (not least at weddings). Central to the repertory and unmistakeably Gallic in idiom, Widor's organ-symphonies were to exert a major influence on organ technique. However, it has been said that they were sometimes guilty of favouring the smaller-scale set piece at the expense of larger-scale symphonic thought. Lacking a sonata design, the seven movements of the First, for instance – a neo-Classical Prelude, a Mendelssohnian Allegretto, an Intermezzo, a Romantic Adagio chorale, a triumphal Marche pontificale, a Meditation, and a closing classical Fugue – add up to not so much a symphony as a diversionary suite.

The 19th-century French organ school streamed, on the one hand, from Benoist (who taught Franck and Saint-Saëns) and, on the other, from Lemmens (who taught Widor and Guilmant). It was Widor's Paris Conservatoire pupils – principally Vierne, Dupré and André Fleury, cream of the French Establishment - who carried on his organ-symphony tradition. Vierne succeeded Widor as organist at the Conservatoire, and later became organist of Notre Dame (where he died). His six symphonies (1899–1930) generally adopt a five-movement layout. Like Widor, Dupré (who taught Messiaen) was both organist at St. Sulpice (1934–71) and a professor at the Conservatoire. 'The World awaiting the Saviour', 'Nativity', 'Crucifixion' and 'Resurrection' make up the four scenes of his Symphonie-Passion (1924). The solo Second Symphony (1929) reverts to a Prelude/Intermezzo/Toccata-type pattern. Fleury, organist at Dijon Cathedral from 1949 to 1971, effectively brought the genre to a close with two four-movement organ-symphonies completed after the Second World War (1947: 1949).

WIDOR PLAYING THE ORGAN AT ST. SULPICE, WHERE HE WAS ORGANIST FROM 1869 TO 1933.

500 Years

OF GREAT ORGAN COMPOSERS

ANTONIO DE CABEZON (Spanish) was born blind. Organist to the court of Spain, his reputation as master composer and charismatic performer was not just a Spanish phenomenon: through his travels abroad, he impressed and influenced as many foreign musicians as he learnt from. His *tientos* Iberianized the Italian *ricercar* style.

GIROLAMO CAVAZZONI (Italian), associated with Venice and Mantua, represented the high point of the 16th-century Italian organ tradition. He left organ masses, hymns and ricercari, and, together with his father, is credited with having written the earliest *canzoni* (based on French *chansons*).

CLAUDIO MERULO (Italian) was the illustrious organist of the cathedrals of Brescia and Parma, as well as St. Mark's, Venice. He formalized the keyboard toccata (pioneered by Andrea Gabrieli) into a glittering succession of alternating display and fugal sections.

JEHAN TITELOUZE (French), organist at Rouen Cathedral from 1588 to 1633, was the first important French composer for the instrument. His late-Renaissance-styled polyphonic *versets* (lit. 'verses') based on plainchant (published in notation, not tablature, 1623, 1626) were intended to alternate with the choir during services.

JAN PIETERSZOON SWEELINCK (Dutch), organist of the Oude Kerk, Amsterdam for more than forty years and one of the most famous teachers of his time. He laid the foundations for Baroque organ style, absorbing elements from the English, French and Italians. His keyboard output included fugal fantasias, variations and toccatas. His influence on the North German 'Gothic' school was considerable.

♪ ST. THOMAS'S, LEIPZIG, A CHURCH SYNONYMOUS WITH THE NAME OF ITS MOST FAMOUS CANTOR, J. S. BACH.

GIROLAMO FRESCOBALDI (Italian) dazzled the courts of Italy, from Ferrara (where he came personally under the influence of Gesualdo, Prince of Venosa) to Mantua and Florence. When he gave his first concert as organist of St Peter's, Rome, it is said that 30,000 people came to hear him. Bach learnt well from his scholarship and art.

SAMUEL SCHEIDT (German), a pupil of Sweelinck, closely linked with the Halle court. He established an Italianate line of German organ writing (chorale variations, fugues, fantasias, magnificats) that led to Bach.

JOHANN JACOB FROBERGER (German), organist to the Viennese court, summed-up the South German style of the Baroque. His discerningly cosmopolitan make-up provocatively acknowledged Italian and French influences (he had been a pupil of Frescobaldi, and was a friend of the French clavecinist Chambonnières).

DIETRICH BUXTEHUDE (Danish/German) Among the guiding stars of the North German school, including the Praetorius family, Buxtehude was the most famous. Organist of the Marienkirche in Lübeck, most of his instrumental music was for organ and included chorale settings and toccatas. Bach as a young man journeyed 200 miles on foot, from Arnstadt to Lübeck, to hear him play.

JUAN BAUTISTA JOSE CABANILLES (Spanish), organist at Valencia Cathedral. His grandly inventive music represented the Baroque culmination of the Iberian tradition founded by Cabezon. "The world will go to ruins before another Cabanilles will arise", lamented one of his pupils.

ANDRE RAISON (French) was one of several major French Baroque organists – together with Clérambault (his pupil, later organist at St Sulpice), Couperin 'le Grand' (organist of St Gervais and organiste du Roi), Daquin (of *Le coucou* fame, organist of Notre Dame), Gigault, Lebègue (*organiste du Roi*), and Marchand (organist of the Cordeliers). Raison's two published collections of organ music, including five masses, are interesting for their notes on performance and for their carefully indicated registrations.

JOHANN PACHELBEL (German) – of *Canon* popularity – epitomized the more easy-going, intimate, uncomplicated surroundings and expectations of the Central German (Thuringian/North Bavarian) school. For a time assistant organist at St Stephen's Cathedral in Vienna, he taught Bach's elder brother. His copious organ music included all the expected genres of the period (chorales, toccatas, preludes, *chaconnes*, *ricercari* and fantasias) but also nearly 100 Magnificat fugues.

JOHANN SEBASTIAN BACH (German) - gatherer of the past, inspirer of the future, a colossus astride history and civilization - was Kantor of St Thomas's, Leipzig. "Lamented Bach!" wrote Telemann, "Your touch upon the organ's keys/Long since has earned you company among the great,/And what your quill upon the music-sheet has writ/Has filled hearts with delight, though some did envy seize". His organ works endure supreme and glorious, as rich in Baroque device as Romantic intensity – though one of them, the popular Toccata and Fugue in D minor, has recently been shown to be not by him.

GEORG FRIDERIC HANDEL (German) was an organist from his youth, enjoying an early appointment at the Calvinist Cathedral in Halle, but apart from his eighteen organ concertos he wrote no other music for the instrument. "I would uncover my head, and kneel down at his tomb," declared Beethoven.

SAMUEL WESLEY (English), a devout admirer of Bach and Handel, was regarded as the greatest English organist of his day, a position inherited by his natural son, Samuel Sebastian Wesley, Anglican organist variously of Hereford, Winchester and Gloucester Cathedrals. Apart from concertos, the bulk of Samuel's organ music took the form of voluntaries for use in church services.

FELIX MENDELSSOHN (German) "There is one god (Bach) and Mendelssohn is his prophet" (Berlioz). Mendelssohn was a key player in the 19th-century Bach Revival movement, and also helped rekindle interest in the organ, stemming its post-Bach decline.

FRANZ LISZT (Hungarian) – Grand Ducal Director of Music Extraordinary to the Weimar court from 1848, champion of

Wagner, Berlioz and Verdi, and defender of the 'New German school' – may have been largely responsible for single-handedly creating modern pianism, but he was also an ambitiously inventive composer for the organ (1850–85), at one stage even planning to write a symphonic poem for the instrument (based on a poem by Herder). His oratorios and settings for the Catholic Church feature it to grand effect.

CESAR FRANCK (Belgian/French), organist of Ste Clothilde and professor of organ at the Paris Conservatoire, was the teacher of d'Indy (founder of the 'New German'-style Schola Cantorum in 1894), Duparc, Chausson, Guilmant and Dukas. He established the Romantic organ school in France (1858–90) at a time when the French organ tradition was particularly impoverished.

ANTON BRUCKNER (Austrian), for a time organist of Linz Cathedral, was celebrated as one of the great organ virtuosos of his day: in 1871, together with Saint-Saëns and others, he helped to inaugurate the large Willis organ of the new Royal Albert Hall in London. But although he wrote for it extensively in his masses, *Te deum* and sacred settings, he left nothing of significance otherwise.

JOHANNES BRAHMS (German), the master classicist of the Romantic age, movingly resurrected the spirit and style of Bach in a set of late Chorale Preludes for organ, published only after his death.

CAMILLE SAINT-SAENS (French), organist of the Madeleine and the teacher of Fauré, was precociously gifted and generously admired – as composer, virtuoso pianist, educator, champion of the Baroque, inquiring ethnomusicologist, poet, critic, Establishment sage. Liszt thought him the greatest organist in the world. Others found him shallow. Initially progressive, latterly conservative, he produced a quantity of organ music from 1886 (the year of his 'Organ' Symphony, No. 3, and *The Carnival of Animals*) to 1919.

ALEXANDRE GUILMANT (French) was organist of the Trinité in Paris, and professor at both the Schola Cantorum and the Conservatoire. His eight sonatas (1874–1906)

are as significant to the French Romantic Cavaillé-Coll organ tradition as the organ-symphonies of Widor and Vierne (qv).

CHARLES-MARIE WIDOR (French), organist of St. Sulpice for over 60 years, dominated Parisian musical life from before Ravel to beyond Fauré. His legacy was the unaccompanied organ-symphony (qv), an original genre taken up by some of his students.

CHARLES TOURNEMIRE (French) studied with Widor and succeeded Franck as organist of Ste. Clothilde. His masterpiece was the *L'orgue mystique* (1932) – 51 organ masses based on plainsong melodies appropiate to different Sundays of the liturgical calendar.

MAX REGER (German) closed the German Romantic organ tradition. Steeped in the magnitude, formal intricacy and polyphony of Bach, Beethoven and Brahms, filtered through the innovation of Liszt, his imposing body of organ music (1898–1913) included chorale fantasias, chorale preludes, fugues, variations, toccatas, sonatas, written-out 'improvisations' and sundry other inventions – all of them characterized by detailed craftsmanship and fastidious attention to detail.

OLIVIER MESSIAEN (French), a pupil of Dupré and Dukas and the teacher of Boulez and Stockhausen, was organist of the Trinité and professor at the Paris Conservatoire from 1941 to 1978. Uniquely personal in sound, rhythmic complexity, source material and religious symbolism, his organ music (1927–86) is profoundly mystical, an extraordinary coming together of the meditative and the ecstatic, of time released and time contained, of centuries-old French organ style absorbed, transcended and reborn.

CHARLES CAMILLERI (Maltese) combines Messiaen's Gallic mysticism with independently imagined rhythms and rituals of a completely different kind - orientally valued, African rooted, New Orleans shadowed. Inspired by the writings of the Jesuit scientist Teilhard de Chardin, his emotionally charged five-movement *Missa Mundi* (1972) towers among the great organ statements of the 20th century.

MISCELLANEOUS KEYBOARDS

Accordion/ Concertina

The 20th-century piano accordion (a 'developed mouth organ') is an air-vacuum or pressure-operated instrument, with freely beating metal reeds - in other words, a portable reed organ. The instrument consists of a pair of rectangular headboards joined by bellows. Power is supplied to the bellows by alternately pushing out (expiration) and then drawing in (inspiration) each end. The right hand plays a piano-style treble keyboard (originally buttons), while the left controls the bellow action and rows of studs governing bass notes and chords. In the hands of a virtuoso player, the accordion can be a dazzling tour-de-force. Roy Harris wrote a concerto for the instrument, and accordion orchestras are common.

The concertina, which was invented seven years after the accordion, in 1829 in England, is smaller and has two studded keyboards, one for each hexagonal casing. On an English concertina the pitches remain constant on extension and compression of the bellows. On German examples, they change. The concertina is considered artistically superior to the accordion, and is more difficult to play. Its greatest early popularizer was the Italian Giulio Regondi, who left concertos, chamber music and many solo pieces. Tchaikovsky used a quartet of concertinas in his Second Orchestral Suite (1883).

With their strong sound and carrying-power, the accordion and concertina have both been widely used in the performance of traditional and open-air music, particularly as an accompaniment to dancing.

Barrel Piano (Street piano)

An upright piano, often without keyboard, operated by a pinned wooden cylinder situated at the bottom of the instrument. The pins of the cylinder, usually configuring several tunes, selectively activated lever arms connected to the hammer mechanism. Popular from the 1850s onwards, frequently with the addition of other instrumental effects, barrel pianos were usually either hand-cranked or spring-wound. Later models were electrically motorized.

Clavicytherium

An upright wing-shaped harpsichord with vertical soundboard, in use until the 18th century. The Royal College of Music in London has a playable example dating from the late 15th century, believed to be the oldest surviving stringed keyboard of any kind.

Claviorganum

A versatile instrument dating from the 16th century, combining a single manual harpsichord (or virginal) with a small organ. Either could be played separately or coupled.

Echiquier (Eschaquier d'Angleterre)

An elusive keyboard instrument of the 14th century onwards, contemporary with the harpsichord and clavichord and often wrongly mistaken for them. Associated with dancing, it was presumably a loud instrument. John I of Aragon (1387) referred to it as "similar to the organ but sounding with strings". Various theories have been pro-

THE PIANO-ACCORDION HAS A SMALL KEYBOARD OF UP TO THREE-AND-A-HALF OCTAVES.

Sostenente
PIANO
℘

Many mechanical attempts, damper pedal apart, have been made to deny the piano its natural attack-decay-release sound character, and to turn it instead into a singing, sustaining hybrid. An early forerunner from the end of the 16th century was the *Clavecin a archet* – a bowed harpsichord with pedalled and cranked rotating rosined wooden wheels functioning as circular bows on the strings.

Following the hurdy-gurdy principle, the harmonichord (1808) favoured a pedalled revolving leather cylinder which came into contact with the strings. Weber wrote an Adagio and Rondo for it. Other initiatives included compressed air (an Aeolian harp with keyboard); rapid hammer repetition (the double-keyboard piano tremolophone, 1842, with one manual controlling the repetition notes); and the piano scande, 1853 (with the hammered string setting free-reeds into vibration).

However, the first convincing *sostenente* instrument, in which the sound can be indefinitely sustained, as on an organ, was not produced until the 1960s when the electric piano made its first appearance.

posed as to what it was: a clavichord with hammer action; an upright harpsichord; an early prototype of a *clavicymbalum*, originating from or associated with England. In a treatise of c.1440, Henri Arnault de Zwolle possibly refers to such an instrument, drawing attention to a mechanism like piano escapement. Nothing has survived.

♪ A LONDON BARREL-PIANO, POPULARLY CALLED A BARREL ORGAN. ITALIAN WORKERS CALLED SUCH INSTRUMENTS 'PIANO-ORGANS'.

℅ Harmonium

A compressed, foot-treadled air reed organ pioneered by Kratzenstein of Copenhagen and Grenie of Paris (patented by Alexandre Debain in 1842). Debain designed wind channels of different size and pressure, which bore on the individual tone-colours of the reeds. Harmon-iums have 'slow speech' (agile music is ineffective), and their sound does not carry well. But they have had their admirers – from Berlioz and Richard Strauss to the Indian outposts of the old British Empire. Dvořák wrote a charming set of *Bagatelles* for harmonium, two violins and cello (1878); and Tchaikovsky stipulates one (not an organ, the usual substitution) for the close of his 'Manfred' Symphony (1885). "The most sensitively and intimately expressive of all instruments," Percy Grainger fervently believed (1929): "... It is unique as a refining musical influence, for it tempts the player to tonal subtleties of gradation as does no other instrument" – sentiments worthy to place beside Mattheson's and C.P.E Bach's endorsement of the clavichord.

℅ Harpsichord-Piano

Combining the plucking jacks of the harpsichord with the hammer action of the piano, these were a late 18th-century fashion, developed in Vienna by Stein and in Paris by Erard.

℅ Melodeon

A suction air reed organ, first manufactured commercially in 1854 by Mason & Hamlin of Boston Massachusetts. Easier to control than the harmonium, though less varied in tone-colour or expression, this was a useful domestic substitute for pipe organ practice. In America the melodeon was known as a 'cabinet organ'; in England as an 'American organ'.

A 'NEW ENGLISH HARMONIUM' OF 1859. THE INSTRUMENT IS 'BLOWN' BY LEFT AND RIGHT FOOT APPLYING PRESSURE ALTERNATELY.

℅ Pedal Piano

A piano fitted with an organ-like pedalboard enabling the bass line to be played with the feet. A 19th-century invention, related functionally to the pedal harpsichord, pedal clavichord and (later) pedal melodeon, it was a useful practice instrument. Mendelssohn and Liszt owned pedal pianos, and Schumann (1845) and Alkan (c. 1869) wrote for it.

℅ Piano Organ

A piano with two or three ranks of pipes, popular with American theatres and funeral parlours up to 1930.

℅ Portable Piano

An "expanding and collapsing piano for gentlemen's yachts, the saloons of steam ships, ladies' cabins etc., only 13 and-a-half inches [34cm] from front to back when collapsed" was shown at the Great Exhibition of 1851. In 1883 a folding harmonium was advertised ' ... being only two feet wide and six inches deep [60 x 15cm]'. Neither fashion caught on.

℅ Reed Organ

The generic label for any keyboard instrument whose sound is generated by metal reed tongues of fixed pitch set in motion by air under compression or suction. Reed organs vary from single to two (or even three) manuals. Air is blown by either foot treadles or motorized electric power. Octave couplers and tremulant devices are usual.

During the 19th century reed organs were as popular domestically as the piano, and were often used in smaller churches in the absence of fixed pipe organs – their modernized, electronic descedents still are. Historically, the technology of the reed organ has its roots in the Chinese *sheng*, or free-reed mouth organ. A simplified form of this instrument became popular all over Europe in the later 18th century, and it is said that the acoustician, inventor and theorist Abbe Vogler (teacher of Weber and Meyerbeer) had encountered an original example in Russia.

℔ *Tastiera per luce*

Invented in 1895 by an Englishman, Wallace Rimington, the 'colour keyboard' or 'colour organ' found lasting fame in the treble stave allocated to it by Scriabin in his *Prometheus, The Poem of Fire* (1908–10). Scriabin adapted Rimington's principle, using a twelve-note keyboard to control the opening and closing of apertures of illuminated tinted glass light intended to bathe the performance in a spectrum of colours according to his own specific key/colour associations (red for C major, bright blue for F sharp, and so on).

Among the many other attempts to wed colour to music and vice versa, typical is Alexander Laszló's *Farblichtklavier* (colour-light keyboard). Laszló's piano compositions are adorned in the score with an additional colour notation which indicates the lights (singly or in combination) which are to glow at given points in the music. He introduced his invention to an audience in 1925 at the German Music Art Festival in Kiel. In addition to Rimington's and Laszló's inventions, several others have been demonstrated, among them later colour organs, in 1912 and 1919, Colour Projector (1921), Clavilux (1922), Musichrome (1932) and Light Console (1934). ℔

Pneumatic Fantasy

℅

COIN PIANO (Nickleodeon) A pneumatically-operated automatic piano triggered by a coin that sets off a mechanical linkage responsible for activating the performing mechanism. Popular in America from before the Great War to Prohibition (1920), coin pianos were considered ideal for relaxed background listening. They flourished everywhere – but, at 25 or 50 cents a two-minute tune, made their best income out of 'sporting house' or brothel money. Speakeasies, too, offered good pickings.

ORCHESTRION A general term describing large self-contained early 20th century pneumatically operated automatic instruments that imitated the sounds of an orchestra. They came in many shapes and sizes (some with keyboards, some without), and used perforated paper-rolls. They enjoyed a vogue in not only (pre-Prohibition) America – where Wurlitzers could come with price tags up to $10,000) but also Europe and England. With origins going back to the Viennese Panharmonican and Orpheusharmonican of Beethoven's time (designed by Maelzel, patentee of the metronome), there were orchestrions to suit any occasion – from playing the classics (the Hupfeld Pan Orchestra), to the latest dance craze and jazz (Hupfeld's Symphony Jazz [with saxophone and lotus flute pipes], the Losche Jazz Band Piano).

PHONOLISZT-VIOLINA Commercialized in 1908 by Hupfeld and later popular in cinemas, this was a pneumatic roll-playing automatic piano with violin (or violins) attached, activated by a circular horsehair bow. *Vibrato*, *glissandi* and muting (*sordino*) were all possible. Efrem Zimbalist called the invention "the eighth wonder and marvel of our time".

PHOTO-PLAYER THEATRE ORGAN An extraordinary altar-piece of the American silent cinema from about 1910 to 1928. Generically, a mechanical keyboard orchestrion or orchestra piano, it took the form of an ornately fanciful twenty-foot wide pneumatic roll-playing automatic orchestra, with a central piano console (complete with pedals, buttons and other controls) framed by cabinets containing various effects. Around 10,000 instruments were manufactured, of which no more than a few dozen survive today. One variant was called a Pipe-organ Orchestra, capable, according to the maker's publicity, of rendering "the tender, true tones of a violin, the brisk notes of a xylophone, the gay click of the castanets, the silver rattle of the tambourine, and the syncopated beats of the drum. He is master of every situation. He is the living interpreter of every shade of emotion registered by the silent players ..."

PIANOLA The basic principle of this self-playing automatic piano was pneumatic leverage to activate the hammers, triggered by a paper-roll of varyingly placed and lengthened perforations corresponding with the pitches and rhythmic durations of a given piece of music. There were two basic types of system. The external, pushed up to a grand or upright piano and aligned, had levered 'fingers' which lay over the keys of the instrument. In its original foot-treadled (pumped) form, 1896, this was known as a Piano Player (popularly Pianola). In its later electrically-motorized cabinet form (c. 1904), equipped with felted wooden 'fingers' and pedal-activating mechanism, it was called a Vorsetzer. The internal (popularized c. 1900), built into the case of the instrument and physically connected with the hammer action, was known as an 'inner player' or Player Piano. The medium was developed further with the appearance of the Reproducing Piano (1904). Patented in Germany, this was an 'expression' instrument, purporting to convey through its mechanics and the digitalized marginelia of its rolls, an artist's tempo, pedalling, touch, phrasing, etc. The big three reproducing pianos were (in Germany) Welte (1905) and (in America) Duo-Art and Ampico (both launched in 1913). Fierce rivals, none of their systems was compatible.

Ensembles

What constitutes an ensemble? It may seem obvious: a musician alone, and the work performed, is called 'solo', yet there is an exception: 18th-century composers wrote 'solos' for one instrument accompanied by at least one other! Thereafter, common sense prevails as we chase numbers: duo, trio, quartet, quintet, sextet, septet, octet, nonet and dectet or decimette. More, and it becomes ensemble (though fewer than eleven might still be called that, or group, or chamber orchestra, so vague is the terminology).

Informally, a 'band' might number from, say, four musicians upwards. Older terms are coming back into vogue – 'Academy' (orchestra), 'Consort' (a group of instruments strictly of the same family; a mixture was a 'broken consort') 'Camerata' (chamber ensemble) and similar names in different languages.

Instrumental groups may be constituted in countless ways. Lyres, lutes and percussion were at the centre of the earliest labour dispute when Aristos (lead lute?) called a strike in Rome about 309 BC because his brothers were missing meal breaks. From AD 1571 to 1642 an ensemble of shawms, recorders, sackbuts and strings gathered in the turret of London's Royal Exchange to play, free, to the populace. No charge was made for the cornett and trombone music sounding from German church towers from the 16th century, the Stadtpfeifer (town pipers) being paid from the rates. Seemingly free, too, were tea-shop trios (usually piano, violin, cello) and café orchestras (violin led) that used to exist in the Western world, though customers paid indirectly.

A charming 18th-century convention, notably in Austria, was the open-air serenade played by wind groups in the streets at evening. These played *Feldparthien* (field works), a term taken from their instruments' earlier military use. In 1755 Moscow heard the first horn band: 37 hunting horns, each player blowing only one note. Extensions followed: groups of up to 60 players; and the radical decision to allow players the luxury of two, or even three, notes. Horn bands spread throughout Europe but are now heard only in enthusiasts' enclaves in Russia.

Early jazz bands consisted of whatever instruments were available, but usually present were piano, banjo, trumpet or cornet, clarinet, trombone and drums. Not all of them played all the time: part of their attraction was the contrasting sounds and moods of solo 'breaks'.

Jazz began before World War I. The Original Dixieland Jazz Band (1916) in New Orleans and Joe 'King' Oliver's Creole Jazz Band (1922) in Chicago, respectively black and white since segregation was practised then, were the first prominent groups to appear. This 'New Orleans Style' became popular all over the States, and early jazz under the catch-all title 'traditional' enjoyed a great resurgence in the 1950s and 1960s as a reaction to the desiccated, esoteric

A CHRONOLOGY OF FAMOUS
Jazz Bands
& THEIR LEADERS

All of the following bands are American except for those of British musicians Chris Barber and John Dankworth.

ORIGINAL DIXIELAND JAZZ BAND Formed 1916: cornet, trombone, clarinet, piano, drums.

BENNIE MOTEN, piano: Trio, 1918; and Kansas City Orchestra, 1923.

DUKE (EDWARD KENNEDY) ELLINGTON, piano: Band, 1921; and His Famous Orchestra, 1927.

(JOE) 'KING' OLIVER, cornet: Creole Jazz Band, 1922; and Dixie Syncopators, 1925.

PAUL WHITEMAN, viola and leader: Orchestra, 1924.

LOUIS ARMSTRONG, trumpet, formed several bands: Hot Five, 1925; Hot Seven, 1927; Savoy Ballroom Five, 1928; Orchestra, 1928?; All-Stars, 1947. He played and sang with many other groups.

'JELLY ROLL' MORTON (Ferdinand Joseph Le Menthe), piano: Red Hot Peppers, 1926.

JIMMY DORSEY, alto sax and clarinet, and Tommy Dorsey, trombone and trumpet, formed the Dorsey Brothers Orchestra, 1928. Tommy formed the Clambake Seven, 1935, to record 'traditional' jazz.

BENNY GOODMAN, clarinet: Band, 1934; re-formed 1940.

'COUNT' (WILLIAM) BASIE, piano: Barons of Rhythm, 1935; Count Basie Orchestra, 1936.

WOODY (WOODROW) HERMAN, clarinet, sax and vocal: Orchestra, 1936; re-formed 1947.

GLENN MILLER, trombone: Orchestra, 1937.

STAN KENTON (Stanley Newcomb), piano and leader: Orchestra, 1940.

DAVE BRUBECK, piano: Octet, 1946; Trio, 1949; Quintet, 1951.

CHRIS BARBER, trombone: Jazz Band, 1949, to play 'traditional' jazz.

JOHN(NY) DANKWORTH, alto sax and clarinet: Seven, 1950; Orchestra, 1953; Quintet, 1982.

MODERN JAZZ QUARTET, 1951: Milt Jackson, vibes; John Lewis, piano; Percy Heath, bass; Kenny Clarke, drums.

sound of 'modern' jazz. By playing in clubs and dance halls, jazz bands earned their keep but had to bear in mind the requirements of dancers to such an extent that the dividing line between jazz and dance music became blurred.

In the late 1930s the Big Band era arrived with Count Basie, the Dorsey Brothers and Glenn Miller – part dance music, part jazz, part progressive, part orchestral. The constitution of these bands ranged from a full orchestra, with brass or strings or reeds predominating, to a group of blown instruments alone, but a strong percussion element, the rhythm section, was

always present. So-called 'modern' jazz emerged in the late 1940s, a sophisticated art, modern chamber music if you will, with limpid textures and progressive approach that acquired cult following. The cool sounds of acoustic guitar, or vibes or flute or alto sax, indeed any instrument or combination, typified the modern jazz idiom.

A constant quest for the new in a bid to attract listeners has led to some strange and not necessarily musically fruitful partnerships, with uncomfortable mixes of jazz and non-Western instruments, and electronic devices with or without 'live' players.

CHAMBER & ENSEMBLES

VIOL CONSORTS, so common in the 16th and 17th centuries, died out early in the 18th century as the violin family took over and wind instruments grew in popularity. Ensemble music was now increasingly linked to the harpsichord, which was employed in three distinct roles: as the leading instrument, in equal partnership with another soloist, or acting as continuo to one or more principal players.

In the wind department the bassoon, surprisingly, was first to be given an important place. In 1621 Dario Castello published a set of *Sonate concertante* in which a treble instrument (?violin) shares responsibilities with bassoon. Trumpet came next, with two sonatas published in 1638 in an instruction book by Girolamo Fantini. An

instruction book (authorship unknown) appeared in 1700 for the oboe; then at last came the first solos for the instrument that was to prove the most popular ensemble workhorse of the 18th century, the flute. Michel de la Barre composed his sonatas for flute and continuo in 1702, but he was so unsure that the flute would become popular that he made them equally suitable for violin. Similarly, William Babell's sonatas (c. 1720) for oboe or violin.

By the mid-18th century wind serenades including oboes, horns, bassoons and even clarinets were common, mainly for open-air use. Indoors, the harpsichord was declining in favour of the fortepiano, and this more powerful instrument formed the kernel of a whole series of genres. In

violin sonatas and so-called piano trios (violin, cello, piano) it took the lion's share of musical material since strings were regarded merely as accompanists, only gradually emerging as contenders in their own right. Piano quartets and quintets also appeared, some with wind instruments, but works for four or five were more regularly written for an 'unbroken' group of strings.

Whereas wind serenades had featured instruments in pairs (two each of oboes, bassoons, horns, for example), a later development tended to use them singly in quintets for flute, oboe, clarinet, bassoon and horn. This combination also appeared occasionally against orchestra in the *Symphonie concertante*, invented in France about 1770.

At one time, orchestral and chamber music had merged (there were 'orchestral trios' and 'orchestral quartets' at Mannheim, playable by small groups or by string orchestras), but by 1800 there was a clear distinction. Beethoven's early string quartets are no more successful when played on full string band than is his Second Symphony in his own arrangement for piano trio. As the 19th century progressed chamber music grew in duration and stature: Dvořák's early string quartets are as long as his symphonies, while Brahms's carefully written piano trios and piano quartets have great depth and intensity of thought.

There was a move towards freedom of instru-

THE ALLEGRI STRING QUARTET IN 1964, WITH CO-FOUNDER ELI GOREN AND PETER THOMAS (VIOLINS), PATRICK IRELAND (VIOLA) AND WILLIAM PLEETH (CELLO).

A RECITAL OF 1760, WITH OBOE, VIOLIN, HORN AND CELLO. NO WORK REQUIRING THIS PRECISE MIX IS KNOWN.

mental deployment, too. Almost any instrument might join the standard string quartet to oblige and honour a famous soloist, and larger groups were catered for as required. Variety was the order of the day. With fewer nobles extending patronage, and financial considerations placing limits on the size of instrumental groups, early 20th-century composers would write to order for any ensemble that happened to be available. This is evident in Prokofiev's 'Overture on Hebrew Themes' (1919) for clarinet, string quartet and piano (he orchestrated it in 1934), and Stravinsky's *Pastorale* (1934) for violin, oboe, English horn, clarinet and bassoon. These odd 'convenience' ensembles, however, hardly equalled the strange combinations of earlier centuries, each, it must be imagined, gathered for special circumstances. Telemann wrote quartets for four violins alone and another for trumpet, two oboes and continuo, but few bettered Johann Ernst Galliard, a German resident in England, who in 1745 produced a sonata for 24 bassoons and four double bassoons.

Chamber Ensembles
TYPES, COMPONENTS AND FAMOUS EXPONENTS

Type	Components	Famous Exponents
FLUTE DUET	(two flutes)	W. F. Bach
FLUTE SONATA	(flute, harpsichord, continuo)	C. P. E. Bach, J. S. Bach, Handel
VIOLIN SONATA:		
TYPE I	(violin, harpsichord, continuo)	Bach, Handel
TYPE II	(keyboard, violin)	Boccherini, Mozart
TYPE III	(violin, piano)	Bartók, Beethoven, Brahms, Grieg, Mendelssohn
CELLO SONATA	(cello, piano)	Beethoven; Brahms
FLUTE TRIO	(flute, violin, continuo)	C. P. E. Bach, J. C. Bach
OBOE TRIO	(2 oboes, bass)	Handel
HORN TRIO	(horn, violin, cello)	Brahms
STRING TRIO	(2 violins, cello)	J. C. Bach, Boccherini
PIANO TRIO	(keyboard, violin, cello)	Beethoven, Boccherini, Brahms, Dvořák, Haydn, Mendelssohn, Mozart, Schubert, Schumann
FLUTE QUARTET	(flute, violin, viola, cello)	J. C. Bach
OBOE QUARTET	(oboe, violin, viola, cello)	Boccherini, Mozart
PIANO QUARTET	(piano, violin, viola, cello)	Brahms, Schumann
STRING QUARTET I	(2 violins, viola, cello)	Bartók, Beethoven, Boccherini, Brahms, Cambini, Dvořák, Haydn, Mendelssohn, Mozart, Schubert, Shostakovich
STRING QUARTET II	(2 violins, cello, double bass)	Rossini
WIND QUINTET:		
TYPE I	(2 clarinets, 2 horns, bassoon)	J. C. Bach
TYPE II	(flute, oboe, clarinet, horn, bassoon)	Cambini, Danzi, Hindemith, Nielsen, Reicha
STRING QUINTET:		
TYPE I	(2 violins, 2 violas, cello)	Boccherini, Brahms, Bruckner, Dvořák, Mendelssohn, Mozart
TYPE II	(2 violins, viola, 2 cellos)	Boccherini, Borodin, Schubert
PIANO QUINTET:		
TYPE I	(piano, 2 violins, viola, cello)	Berwald, Boccherini, Brahms, Dvořák, Schumann
TYPE II	(piano, violin, viola, cello, bass)	Schubert
PIANO AND WIND QUINTET	(piano, oboe, clarinet, horn, bassoon)	Beethoven, Mozart
WIND SEXTET	(various combinations)	Beethoven, Haydn, Mozart,
STRING SEXTET	(2 violins, 2 violas, 2 cellos)	Boccherini, Brahms, Pleyel, Dvořák, Tchaikovsky
MIXED SEXTET		Beethoven, Boccherini
WIND SEPTET		Janáček
MIXED SEPTET	(clarinet, bassoon, horn, violin, viola, cellos, bass)	Berwald
WIND OCTET		Beethoven, Hummel, Krommer
MIXED OCTET		Boccherini, Schubert
STRING OCTET		Mendelssohn, Spohr
WIND NONET		Krommer
WIND DECTET		Krommer, Spohr

THE EARLY ORCHESTRA

THE RISE OF THE ORCHESTRA has been closely tied to developments in the world of opera. Even the name 'orchestra' originated in the opera house. It dates from Ancient Greece, when theatrical productions often involved music in some form, and the word *orkhéstra* denoted the space in front of the stage used by the singing and dancing chorus. The first operas were intended to imitate that early Greek style of theatre, so it seemed quite natural to Renaissance musicians to apply the name 'orchestra' to the ensemble that now occupied the space once used by the chorus.

As the popularity of opera grew during the 17th century, composers realized that instruments needed to do more than simply accompany the singing and that they should express the thoughts and emotions of the characters. So instruments used for opera performances became the first to be sorted into groups with distinct roles – in other words, an orchestra. In Monteverdi's *Orfeo* (1607), the first real opera, one group of instruments stands out, the strings, including the newly invented violin which was capable of a more powerful sound than its predecessors, the viols. Violins soon came to be accepted as effective concert instruments, and by

the mid-1600s Monteverdi's use of an orchestra comprising strings and harp was regarded as a benchmark. Equally influential was the court of Louis XIV in France, particularly with the appointment in 1653 of Jean-Baptiste Lully as composer-in-chief. The court's influence throughout Europe was considerable. With Louis' 24 'Violons' or 'Grande Bande' at his disposal, as well as the oboes and bassoons of the

THE MAKE-UP OF
Early Orchestral Forces

FOR MONTEVERDI'S *ORFEO*

When Monteverdi scored his opera he was very specific about the instruments he required, unusually so for the time. His large orchestra of 1607 was made up as follows: 4 violins, 4 violas, 2 cellos, 2 double basses, 3 viols, 2 flutes, 4 trumpets and 2 cornetts, 4 trombones, 6 keyboards and 6 plucked strings and drums (?).

THE '24 VIOLONS DU ROI'

The band of 24 strings in the court of Louis XIV of France was more typical of the day. When used by Lully for his operas it was often supplemented by instruments from the king's 12 *Grandes Hautbois* and other miscellaneous instruments as necessary. A typical example from the 1670s would be: 6 violins, 12 violas, 6 cellos, 2 flutes, 2 oboes, 1 bassoon, 2 trumpets, 1 drum, 1 keyboard.

AMATEUR BAROQUE ORCHESTRA

During the Baroque period it was just as common to hear a group of amateur players gathered together to form an informal orchestra as it was to hear one in an opera house. In 1770 the music historian Charles Burney recorded the make-up of a typical Italian amateur orchestra as follows:

"There were 12 or 14 performers: several good violins; two German [transverse] flutes, a violoncello and a small double bass."

FOR HANDEL'S OPERAS

Handel moved to London around 1710, and by the late 1720s was promoting opera performances at the King's Theatre, London, towards the end of what had been a very successful career as an opera composer in England. At that time an orchestra for his operas probably took the following form, with one of the earliest uses of the French horn in England: 22 violins, 2 violas, 3 cellos, 2 double basses, 2 flutes, 2 oboes, 3 bassoons, 2 horns, 2 keyboards, 1 plucked string.

MANNHEIM COURT ORCHESTRA

The famous orchestra at Mannheim exerted considerable influence in establishing the standard Classical orchestra. In the 1770s the orchestra there consisted of the following: 20 violins, 4 violas, 4 cellos, 4 double basses 3 flutes, 3 oboes, 3 clarinets, 4 bassoons, 4 horns, 2 trumpets, 1 timpani, 1 keyboard.

AN OPERATIC SCENE OF THE 1760S THOUGHT TO BE FROM A 'TURKISH' OPERA BY GLUCK.

12 *Grandes Hautbois*, Lully was able to establish the first real orchestral ensembles.

By the late 17th century, almost all the instruments now associated with the orchestra were available for use, but the strings retained their prominence. The melody and bass line of a piece of music were still the most important, and these were taken by the upper and lower strings while the middle parts were filled by 'continuo' instruments. The continuo remained important throughout the first half of the 18th century, and even in the early 19th century a keyboard was often found holding the harmony of orchestral music together. In Mozart's piano concertos, for example, the composer expected the pianist to play a continuo during the *tutti* sections as well as the solo parts.

During the 1700s writers like Quantz and Rousseau expressed differing views on the proper make-up of an orchestra. Strings and continuo, plus woodwinds and sometimes brass, was a generally accepted formula, but difficulties of travel and communication meant that ensembles were rarely consistent except in the most basic outline. Gradually, as international communication improved, the qualities of those orchestras benefitting from better organization came to be appreciated more widely. One of the most influential of these orchestras was that of Duke Carl Theodor at Mannheim. It was established in the 1740s by his *Kapellmeister*, Johann Stamitz, who was encouraged to engage musicians from all over Europe. As the skills of performing and composing often went hand-in-hand at this time, many of the players in the Mannheim orchestra were also accomplished composers. Among the advancements made at Mannheim were an attention to musical phrasing, the idea of uniform bowing for each string section and the techniques of *crescendo* and *diminuendo*, and the famous 'Mannheim rocket' of ascending *tutti* crotchets. The Mannheim orchestra also pioneered the replacement of improvised continuo with written-out parts.

THE MODERN ORCHESTRA

Brian's 'GOTHIC' SYMPHONY

℆

At a time when composers were leaving behind the mighty orchestras demanded by some late-Romantic scores, and the Depression was causing the depletion of musical forces everywhere, Havergal Brian produced the first of his output of 32 symphonies, the Symphony No. 1, written between 1919 and 1927. This 90-minute work is constructed in two parts, with each part composed of three movements. The *Te Deum* setting that constitutes Part Two requires forces of unparalleled scale. These are listed below and include those instruments doubled by existing players:

- 2 piccolos, 6 flutes, alto flute, 6 oboes, oboe d'amore, bass oboe, 2 cor anglais
- 2 E flat and 5 B flat clarinets, 2 basset horns, 2 bass clarinets, pedal clarinet
- 3 bassoons, 2 contrabassoons, 8 horns, 2 E flat cornets, 8 trumpets, bass trumpet
- 3 tenor trombones, 1 bass trombone, 2 contrabass trombones, 2 euphoniums, 2 tubas
- 2 sets of timpani, 2 harps, organ, celesta
- Other percussion, including: glockenspiel, xylophone, 2 bass drums, 6 large pairs of cymbals, tubular bells, bird scare, thunder machine
- Strings
- Soprano, alto, tenor and bass soloists, 2 large choruses, children's chorus
- Plus 4 brass bands each comprising 2 horns, 2 trumpets, 2 tenor trombones, 2 tubas and a set of timpani.

DURING THE 19th century the orchestra underwent astonishing growth. Particularly influential in this were the revolutionary changes that the woodwind and brass families were subject to during the 1800s. In the later symphonies composed by Mozart and Haydn clarinets had become an integral part of the woodwind section, and now other instruments began to be added. These included the piccolo, trombone and contrabassoon in symphonies by Beethoven, and the cor anglais and bass clarinet in music by Berlioz and Meyerbeer respectively. However, it was Richard Wagner, more than any other 19th-century composer, who changed the constitution of the orchestra. Not content with merely accepting what was available to him, he wrote for vastly extended forces and was even prone to inventing new instruments when the particular sound he wanted was not immediately achievable. In writing for such large orchestras, Wagner set the pace for late-Romantic composers like Strauss and Schoenberg, who, at least until World War I, behaved as if they thought the orchestra would continue to develop in size.

By the 1920s this extravagance had lost favour. Composers began to experiment with smaller ensembles, some even making a deliberate return to the modestly proportioned orchestras of earlier generations (Prokofiev, for example, in his 'Classical' Symphony of 1917). In a situation remarkably similar to what had occurred in opera's infancy, composers were now prepared to score works according to what was available to them, or to use existing forces in new and interesting ways. Stravinsky, for example, in his *Symphony of Psalms* (1930) used an orchestra without any violins or violas. The percussion section, in particular, grew in size and importance as composers experimented with increasingly complex rhythms.

Generally speaking, today's orchestra corresponds in size to that of the late 19th century. It is big enough to cope with most of the larger late-Classical and Romantic works and flexible enough to present authentically-scored performances of music by Mozart or Schubert. Other than strings, the usual constituents of a modern orchestra are three flutes (one doubling piccolo), three oboes (one doubling cor anglais), three clarinets (one doubling bass clarinet), three bassoons (one doubling contrabassoon), four horns, three trumpets, three trombones and a tuba. Also common are two harps in addition to a set of timpani and a range of other percussion. Among other 'instruments' occasionally added to the 20th-century orchestra have been typewriters, anvils, chains, wine glasses, the wind machine (often used to represent the breathing scored in the 'birth to death' journey of Tippett's Fourth Symphony, 1977), and the electronic *ondes*

martenot, whose unearthly sound makes a remarkable addition to the orchestra in Messiaen's *Turangalîla-symphonie* (1948).

Where economic or other factors have forced limitations on orchestral size, some musicians have established permanent groups of leaner proportions that are particularly suited to a great deal of music written since World War I. Among many such ensembles, two of particular note are the Basle and Zürich Chamber Orchestras, established by Paul Sacher in the years between the two world wars and responsible for commissioning music from some of the century's leading composers, including Bartók, Berio, Henze, Stravinsky and Tippett. Also notable is the Orpheus Chamber Orchestra which, though apparently unusual in performing without a conductor, reminds us that the conductor in the form now familiar to us did not appear until the early 19th century. (Many orchestral musicians aver

that conductors are, at best, a mixed blessing!)

While the modern orchestra's principal purpose remains to perform concerts, many groups also recognize their importance as a community resource. Increasingly, the job of an orchestra is to take the music to the people, rather than simply expecting the people to come to the music. This often takes the form of music workshops or small-scale performances in local community venues and schools. Increasingly, an orchestra's outreach programme is now seen as a core part of its artistic activity. It is a far cry from the early days of the orchestra when access to its performances was largely restricted to a privileged few.

WRITING FOR THE ORCHESTRA

THE ORCHESTRA'S CAPACITY to produce an homogenous sound in performance can be explained by the complex balancing act that lies at the heart of successful composition. As the orchestra developed from its early days of purely strings, or strings doubled by woodwind, composers were often highly circumspect when it came to adding new instruments. Only those instruments thought suitable for orchestral performance were included, and then only in appropriate quantities. The composer's skill has always been as much concerned with achieving the correct instrumental balance for the desired effect as it has been with simply getting the notes right.

The standard modern orchestra mixes everything in moderation, according to the relative strengths of the instrumental 'voices' at its disposal. The result is a natural homogeneity that gives the composer a head start. The real skill of writing for orchestra, or 'orchestration' as the discipline is usually called, is in moulding the constituent parts of the ensemble in such a way as to produce constantly varied and interesting results, without losing essential elements of the music in a mêlée.

To a greater or lesser extent composers have always been interested in the sound effect of individual instruments. However, it is only quite recently that the art of blending and balancing those instruments has received serious consideration. Trumpets have always had an association with the battlefield and horns with hunting, while in early opera the double bass was commonly

𝄞 IGOR STRAVINSKY, ONE OF THE 20TH-CENTURY'S MOST IMAGINATIVE ORCHESTRATORS.

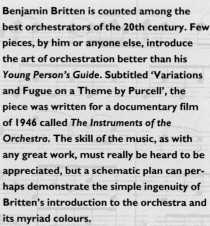

BENJAMIN BRITTEN (LEFT), MASTER OF ORCHESTRATION, SITS IN AT A REHEARSAL IN 1976.

reserved for storm or earthquake scenes. Towards the end of the 18th century, however, the first masters of orchestration emerged. Chief among them was Mozart. In his symphonies and piano concertos he developed dialogues between the sections of the orchestra, including the soloist in the concertos, resulting in constantly shifting instrumental colour that was previously unknown.

For all the myriad directives laid down in text books, not least Berlioz's *Treatise on Instrumentation and Orchestration* (1843), the basic skills required have not changed. Essentially orchestration is about understanding the sound of individual instruments, their place in the grand scheme of the orchestra, and how successfully or otherwise they might be paired with other instruments. Even in the 1770s, for instance, it was understood that an ensemble of strings, woodwind and horns would, in the normal course of events, not present any serious deficiencies in balance. However, to add trumpeters to it, who at that stage habitually occupied the upper reaches of their compass, might upset the status quo. So trumpeters lost their high florid parts, and found themselves restricted to more mundane material in the lower registers.

Not surprisingly, the strength of the body of strings in an early orchestra did not approach that in a modern ensemble, and woodwind instruments have since developed greater power, too. Today the appreciation of how instruments may be mixed is far in advance of what it was in these early ensembles. Extremes of register are known to sit quite happily together in the right context. A low flute passage, for example, might be particularly affecting, but it would also be drowned out easily unless employed at a quiet moment. Likewise a high, piercing trumpet part will readily dominate strings and woodwind.

For all their skill in shaping the sound of the orchestra, composers have from time to time asked the impossible of their players, often without shame. On being told that his Violin Concerto would need a player with six fingers, Schoenberg is reputed to have replied, "I can wait!" Usually, though, asking a great deal of performers is a natural result of experimentation with musical form. Certainly, without occasionally stretching the capabilities of an instrument or the technique of a player, few advancements would be made.

In the final analysis, though, only so much about orchestration can be learned from a secondary source. The best way to acquire the skill, as composers have found since time immemorial, is to listen with a critical ear. This will always be the best tutor. ⟨B⟩

Orchestration
A MUSICAL GUIDE
℅

Benjamin Britten is counted among the best orchestrators of the 20th century. Few pieces, by him or anyone else, introduce the art of orchestration better than his *Young Person's Guide*. Subtitled 'Variations and Fugue on a Theme by Purcell', the piece was written for a documentary film of 1946 called *The Instruments of the Orchestra*. The skill of the music, as with any great work, must really be heard to be appreciated, but a schematic plan can perhaps demonstrate the simple ingenuity of Britten's introduction to the orchestra and its myriad colours.

PART ONE – THEME
Played section by section: woodwind, brass, strings, percussion

PART TWO – VARIATIONS
Instruments present variations on the theme in an array of different groupings, including:
~ **flutes and harp, with *tremolo* strings.**
~ **bassoons with *sforzando* string chords.**
~ ***staccato* wind and brass chords, moving from the top of the range to the bottom.**
~ **tam-tam and harp, over shimmering strings.**
~ **side-drum and trumpets in a *galop*.**
~ **strings and percussion, notably timpani and xylophone, but also castanets and whip.**

PART THREE – FUGUE
Each section joins in the fugue, starting with the highest instrument and working to the lowest, where appropriate, in the following order: woodwind, strings, harp, brass and percussion.

INDEX

KEYBOARD INSTRUMENTS AND ENSEMBLES

Keyboard Instruments and Ensembles

The publishers would like to thank the following sources for their kind
permission to reproduce the pictures in this book:

AKG London, Courtesy Bösendorfer/Stefan Jakubowski, The Bridgeman
Art Library, Corbis, Mary Evans Picture Library, Finchcocks Collection,
Goudhurst, Kent, Hulton Getty/Auerbach, The Lebrecht
Collection/Luckhurst , W. Suschitzky, National Trust Photographic
Library, Popperfoto, Steinway & Sons, Courtesy Yamaha

About the Author

Robert Dearling is a respected classical music writer and reviewer. In addition to being a specialist in the music of the 18th century, he has considerable knowledge of musical instruments and over the past 30 years has amassed a huge database of information pertaining to the histories and uses of the world's instruments. He has a wide knowledge of music journalism and has written for many periodicals. He has also written over 400 sleeve and CD booklet notes for among others, Decca, EMI, RCA and Sony. His books include *The Guinness Book of Music*, *The Guinness Book of Recorded Sound*, and *Mozart – The Symphonies*.